GOD'S POWER THROUGH PRAYER

God's Power Through Prayer

Published by:
J. Countryman Publishers
P.O. Box 90776
Houston, Texas 77290
Telephone: (713) 893-1050

Production Agency
Marketing Communications Graphics, Inc.
9029 Directors Row
Dallas, Texas 75247
Telephone: (214) 630-4300

ISBN: 0-937347-02-7

Printed in Belgium

Contents

I. Amazing Answers To Prayer

Abraham 20
Jacob 13
Rachel 14
Israel 15
Moses 15
Joshua 17
Samson ....
Gideon 18
Manoah 18
Hannah 19
David 20
Elijah 20
Elisha 21
Jabez 21
Jeroboam 22
Hezekiah 22
Daniel 23
Jonah ....
Simeon 25
Jesus 25
Thief on the Cross ....
Peter ....
Paul ....

II. Intercessory Prayer

Jesus' Intercession For Us 37
Our Intercession for Others 39
The Holy Spirit in Intercession 39

III. Great Intercessors

Jesus Christ 54
Paul 61

Contents

I. Amazing Answers To Prayer

Abraham 10
Jacob 13
Rachel 14
Israel 14
Moses 15
Joshua 17
Samson 17
Gideon 18
Manoah 18
Hannah 19
David 20
Elijah 20
Elisha 21
Jabez 21
Jeroboam 22
Hezekiah 22
Daniel 23
Jonah 24
Simeon 25
Jesus 25
Thief on the Cross 33
Peter 33
Paul 34

II. Intercessory Prayer

Jesus' Intercession for Us 37
Our Intercession for Others 39
The Holy Spirit in Intercession 49

III. Great Intercessors

Jesus Christ 54
Paul 61

Jehoshaphat 67
Ezra 69
Zacharias 69
Hezekiah 70
Jeremiah 71
Moses 73
Jacob 74
Mary 75
Daniel 76
Cornelius 78
Abraham 79
Hosea 81
Isaac 81
Job 81
Manasseh 82
Hannah 82
Nehemiah 84

IV. Prayer Promises

Prayer for Others 87
Prayer for Spiritual Healing 101
Prayer for Physical Healing 116
God's Gifts of Prosperity 122
Promise of Revival 135
Prayer for Guidance 139

V. Preparation for Prayer

Meditation in God's Word 145
Ministering to God 150
Fasting 152
Praise 158
Thanksgiving 169

VI. Attitudes for Prayer

Forgiveness 173
Obedience 176

Sincerity 180
Humility 182
Purity. 184
Joy 188

VII. Conditions for Prayer

Praying in the Word 191
Praying in Faith 195
Praying in the Spirit 206
Hindrances to Prayer 208

VIII. Spiritual Warfare Through Prayer

Authority of the Name of Jesus 215
Persistance and Prevailing in Prayer 219
Petitions and Patterns for Prayer 230
Agreement in Prayer 242

IX. Praying in the Psalms

God's Provision 255
God's Protection. 255
Praise to the Lord 257
Our Preservation 258
Our Comfort. 259
God's Sovereignty 260
God's Strength 261
Our Protection 263
God's Compassion 266
Our Yearning for the Lord 268
God's Power, Presence, and Peace 270
God's Forgiveness 272
Our Petitions. 274
God's Greatness 276
God's Mercy. 283
God's Purity 287
Our Purity. 289

Amazing Answers to Prayer...

PRAYER: Abraham for a child

And Abram said, Lord God, what wilt thou give me, seeing I go childless, and the steward of my house is this Eliezer of Damascus?

And he brought him forth abroad, and said, Look now toward heaven, and tell the stars, if thou be able to number them: and he said unto him, So shall thy seed be.

And he believed in the Lord; and he counted it to him for righteousness.

Genesis 15:2, 5, 6

ANSWER

And the Lord visited Sarah as he had said, and the Lord did unto Sarah as he had spoken.

For Sarah conceived, and bare Abraham a son in his old age, at the set time of which God had spoken to him.

And Abraham called the name of his son that was born unto him, whom Sarah bare to him, Isaac.

Genesis 21:1-3

PRAYER: Abraham intercedes for Sodom

And Abraham drew near, and said, Wilt thou also destroy the righteous with the wicked?

Peradventure there be fifty righteous within the city: wilt thou also destroy and not spare the place for the fifty righteous that are therein?

That be far from thee to do after this manner, to slay the righteous with the wicked: and that the righteous should be as the wicked, that be far from thee: Shall not the Judge of all the earth do right?

And the Lord said, If I find in Sodom fifty righteous within the city, then I will spare all the place for their sakes.

And Abraham answered and said, Behold now, I have taken upon me to speak unto the Lord, which am but dust and ashes:

Peradventure there shall lack five of the fifty righteous: wilt thou destroy all the city for lack of five? And he said, If I find there forty and five, I will not destroy it.

And he spake unto him yet again, and said, Peradventure there shall be forty found there. And he said, I will not do it for forty's sake.

And he said unto him, Oh let not the Lord be angry, and I will speak: Peradventure there shall thirty be found there. And he said, I will not do it, if I find thirty there.

And he said, Behold now, I have taken upon me to speak unto the Lord: Peradventure there shall be twenty found there. And he said, I will not destroy it for twenty's sake.

And he said, Oh let not the Lord be angry, and I will speak yet but this once: Peradventure ten shall be found there. And he said, I will not destroy it for ten's sake.

And the Lord went his way, as soon as he had left communing with Abraham: and Abraham returned unto his place.

Genesis 18:23-33

ANSWER

And it came to pass, when God destroyed the cities of the plain, that God remembered Abraham, and sent Lot out of the midst of the overthrow, when he overthrew the cities in the which Lot dwelt.

Genesis 19:29

PRAYER: Abraham's confidence in God

And Abraham said, My son, God will provide himself a lamb for a burnt offering: so they went both of them together.

Genesis 22:8

ANSWER

And Abraham lifted up his eyes, and looked, and behold behind him a ram caught in a thicket by his horns: and Abraham went and took the ram, and offered him up for a burnt offering in the stead of his son.

Genesis 22:13

PRAYER: Abraham prays for Isaac's wife

And Abraham said unto his eldest servant of his house, that ruled over all that he had, Put, I pray thee, thy hand under my thigh:

And I will make thee swear by the Lord, the God of heaven, and the God of earth, that thou shalt not take a wife unto my son of the daughters of the Canaanites, among whom I dwell:

But thou shalt go unto my country, and to my kindred, and take a wife unto my son Isaac.

Genesis 24:2-4

ANSWER

Behold, Rebekah is before thee, take her, and go, and let her be thy master's son's wife, as the Lord hath spoken.

Genesis 24:51

PRAYER: Jacob prays for deliverance

And Jacob said, O God of my father Abraham, and God of my father Isaac, the LORD which saidst unto me, Return unto thy country, and to thy kindred, and I will deal well with thee:

Deliver me, I pray thee, from the hand of my brother, from the hand of Esau: for I fear him, lest he will come and smite me, and the mother with the children.

Genesis 32:9, 11

ANSWER: And thou saidst, I will surely do thee good, and make thy seed as the sand of the sea, which cannot be numbered for multitude.

Genesis 32:12

PRAYER: Rachel prays for a child

And when Rachel saw that she bare Jacob no children, Rachel envied her sister; and said unto Jacob, Give me children, or else I die.

And Jacob's anger was kindled against Rachel: and he said, Am I in God's stead, who hath withheld from thee the fruit of the womb?

Genesis 30:1, 2

ANSWER

And God remembered Rachel, and God hearkened to her, and opened her womb.

And she conceived, and bare a son; and said, God hath taken away my reproach:

And she called his name Joseph; and said, The Lord shall add to me another son.

Genesis 30:22-24

PRAYER: Israel cries for deliverance

And it came to pass in process of time, that the king of Egypt died: and the children of Israel sighed by reason of the bondage, and they cried, and their cry came up unto God by reason of the bondage.

Exodus 2:23

ANSWER

And God heard their groaning, and God remembered his covenant with Abraham, with Isaac, and with Jacob.

And God looked upon the children of Israel, and God had respect unto them.

Exodus 2:24-25

PRAYER: Moses prays for grace

Remember Abraham, Isaac, and Israel, thy servants, to whom thou swarest by thine own self, and saidst unto them, I will multiply your seed as the stars of heaven, and all this land that I have spoken of will I give unto your seed, and they shall inherit it for ever.

Exodus 32:13

ANSWER

Nevertheless he regarded their affliction, when he heard their cry;

And he remembered for them his covenant, and repented according to the multitude of his mercies.

Psalm 106:44, 45

PRAYER: Moses prays for glory

And he said, I beseech thee, shew me thy glory.

Exodus 33:18

ANSWER

And he said, I will make all my goodness pass before thee, and I will proclaim the name of the Lord before thee; and will be gracious to whom

I will be gracious, and will shew mercy on whom I will shew mercy.

Exodus 33:19

PRAYER: Moses prays for the scattering of enemies

And they departed from the mount of the Lord three days' journey: and the ark of the covenant of the Lord went before them in the three days' journey, to search out a resting place for them.

And the cloud of the Lord was upon them by day, when they went out of the camp.

And it came to pass, when the ark set forward, that Moses said, Rise up, Lord, and let thine enemies be scattered; and let them that hate thee flee before thee.

And when it rested, he said, Return, O Lord, unto the many thousands of Israel.

Numbers 10:33-36

ANSWER

And when the people complained, it displeased the Lord: and the Lord heard it; and his anger was kindled; and the fire of the Lord burnt among them, and consumed them that were in the uttermost parts of the camp.

And the people cried unto Moses; and when Moses prayed unto the Lord, the fire was quenched.

Numbers 11:1, 2

PRAYER: Joshua - That the sun stand still
Then spake Joshua to the Lord in the day when the Lord delivered up the Amorites before the children of Israel, and he said in the sight of Israel, Sun, stand thou still upon Gibeon; and thou, Moon, in the valley of Ajalon.

Joshua 10:12

ANSWER
And the sun stood still, and the moon stayed, until the people had avenged themselves upon their enemies. Is not this written in the book of Jasher? So the sun stood still in the midst of heaven, and hasted not to go down about a whole day.

Joshua 10:13

PRAYER: Samson prays for strength
And Samson called unto the Lord, and said, O Lord God, remember me, I pray thee, and strengthen me, I pray thee, only this once, O God, that I may be at once avenged of the Philistines for my two eyes.

Judges 16:28

ANSWER
And Samson took hold of the two middle pillars upon which the house stood, and on which it was borne up, of the one with his right hand, and of the other with his left.

And Samson said, Let me die with the Philistines. And he bowed himself with all his might; and the house fell upon the lords, and upon all the people that were therein. So the dead which he slew at his death were more than they which he slew in his life.

Judges 16:29, 30

PRAYER: Gideon prays for a fleece

And Gideon said unto God, Let not thine anger be hot against me, and I will speak but this once: let me prove, I pray thee, but this once with the fleece; let it now be dry only upon the fleece, and upon all the ground let there be dew.

Judges 6:39

ANSWER

And God did so that night: for it was dry upon the fleece only, and there was dew on all the ground.

Judges 6:40

PRAYER: Manoah prays for his child

And God hearkened to the voice of Manoah; and the angel of God came again unto the woman as she sat in the field: but Manoah her husband was not with her.

Judges 13:9

ANSWER

For it came to pass, when the flame went up toward heaven from off the altar, that the angel of the Lord ascended in the flame of the altar. And Manoah and his wife looked on it, and fell on their faces to the ground.

And the woman bare a son, and called his name Samson: and the child grew, and the Lord blessed him.

Judges 13:20, 24

PRAYER: Hannah asks for Samuel

And she was in bitterness of soul, and prayed unto the Lord, and wept sore.

And she vowed a vow, and said, O Lord of hosts, if thou wilt indeed look on the affliction of thine handmaid, and remember me, and not forget thine handmaid, but wilt give unto thine handmaid a man child, then I will give him unto the Lord all the days of his life, and there shall no razor come upon his head.

I Samuel 1:10, 11

ANSWER

Wherefore it came to pass, when the time was come about after Hannah had conceived, that she bare a son, and called his name Samuel, saying, Because I have asked him of the Lord.

I Samuel 1:20

PRAYER: David kills Goliath

Then said David to the Philistine, Thou comest to me with a sword, and with a spear, and with a shield: but I come to thee in the name of the Lord of hosts, the God of the armies of Israel, whom thou hast defied.

I Samuel 17:45

ANSWER

So David prevailed over the Philistine with a sling and with a stone, and smote the Philistine, and slew him; but there was no sword in the hand of David.

I Samuel 17:50

PRAYER: Elijah prays for fire

Hear me, O Lord, hear me, that this people may know that thou art the Lord God, and that thou hast turned their heart back again.

I Kings 18:37

ANSWER

Then the fire of the Lord fell, and consumed the burnt sacrifice, and the wood, and the stones, and the dust, and licked up the water that was in the trench.

I Kings 18:38

PRAYER: Elisha prays for Shunammite's son

And when Elisha was come into the house, behold, the child was dead, and laid upon his bed.

He went in therefore, and shut the door upon them twain, and prayed unto the Lord.

II Kings 4:32, 33

ANSWER

Then he returned, and walked in the house to and fro; and went up, and stretched himself upon him: and the child sneezed seven times, and the child opened his eyes.

II Kings 4:35

PRAYER: Jabez prays for blessing

And Jabez called on the God of Israel, saying, Oh that thou wouldest bless me indeed, and enlarge my coast, and that thine hand might be with me, and that thou wouldest keep me from evil, that it may not grieve me!

I Chronicles 4:10

ANSWER

And God granted him that which he requested.

I Chronicles 4:10

PRAYER: King Jeroboam asks for healing

And the king answered and said unto the man of God, Entreat now the face of the Lord thy God, and pray for me, that my hand may be restored me again.

I Kings 13:6

ANSWER

And the man of God besought the Lord, and the king's hand was restored him again, and became as it was before.

I Kings 13:6b

PRAYER: Hezekiah prays for healing

Then he turned his face to the wall, and prayed unto the Lord, saying,

I beseech thee, O Lord, remember now how I have walked before thee in truth and with a perfect heart, and have done that which is good in thy sight. And Hezekiah wept sore.

II Kings 20:2, 3

ANSWER

Turn again, and tell Hezekiah the captain of my people, Thus saith the Lord, the God of David thy father, I have heard thy prayer, I have seen thy tears: behold, I will heal thee: on the third day thou shalt go up unto the house of the Lord.

And Isaiah said, Take a lump of figs. And they took and laid it on the boil, and he recovered.

II Kings 20:5, 7

PRAYER: Daniel prays

Now when Daniel knew that the writing was signed, he went into his house; and his windows being open in his chamber toward Jerusalem, he kneeled upon his knees three times a day, and prayed, and gave thanks before his God, as he did aforetime.

Daniel 6:10

ANSWER

Then the king commanded, and they brought Daniel, and cast him into the den of lions. Now the king spake and said unto Daniel, Thy God whom thou servest continually, he will deliver thee.

Then said Daniel unto the king, O king, live for ever.

My God hath sent his angel, and hath shut the lions' mouths, that they have not hurt me: forasmuch as before him innocency was found in me; and also before thee, O king, have I done no hurt.

Daniel 6:16, 21, 22

PRAYER: Daniel prays for revelation

And I set my face unto the Lord God, to seek by prayer and supplications, with fasting, and sackcloth, and ashes:

And I prayed unto the Lord my God, and made my confession, and said, O Lord, the great and dreadful God, keeping the covenant and mercy to them that love him, and to them that keep his commandments;

Daniel 9:3, 4

ANSWER

And whiles I was speaking, and praying, and confessing my sin and the sin of my people Israel, and presenting my supplication before the Lord my God for the holy mountain of my God;

Yea, whiles I was speaking in prayer, even the man Gabriel, whom I had seen in the vision at the beginning, being caused to fly swiftly, touched me about the time of the evening oblation.

And he informed me, and talked with me, and said, O Daniel, I am now come forth to give thee skill and understanding.

Daniel 9:20-22

PRAYER: Jonah prays

Then Jonah prayed unto the Lord his God out of the fish's belly.

Jonah 2:1

ANSWER

When my soul fainted within me I remembered the Lord: and my prayer came in unto thee, into thine holy temple.

And the Lord spake unto the fish, and it vomited out Jonah upon the dry land.

Jonah 2:7, 10

PRAYER: Simeon waits for the Christ

And, behold, there was a man in Jerusalem, whose name was Simeon; and the same man was just and devout, waiting for the consolation of Israel: and the Holy Ghost was upon him.

And it was revealed unto him by the Holy Ghost, that he should not see death, before he had seen the Lord's Christ.

Luke 2:25, 26

ANSWER

Lord, now lettest thou thy servant depart in peace, according to thy word:

For mine eyes have seen thy salvation.

Luke 2:29, 30

PRAYER: Restoration of Peter's mother-in-law

And when Jesus was come into Peter's house, he saw his wife's mother laid, and sick of a fever.

Matthew 8:14

ANSWER

And he touched her hand, and the fever left her: and she arose, and ministered unto them.

Matthew 8:15

PRAYER: Healing of issue of blood

For she said within herself, If I may but touch his garment I shall be whole.

Matthew 9:21

ANSWER

But Jesus turned him about, and when he saw her, he said, Daughter, be of good comfort; thy faith hath made thee whole. And the woman was made whole from that hour.

Matthew 9:22

PRAYER: Healing of blind men

And when Jesus departed thence, two blind men followed him, crying, and saying, Thou Son of David, have mercy on us.

Matthew 9:27

ANSWER

Then touched he their eyes, saying, According to your faith be it unto you.

Matthew 9:29

PRAYER: The feeding of the five thousand

And he commanded the multitude to sit down on the grass, and took the five loaves, and the two fishes, and looking up to heaven, he blessed, and brake, and gave the loaves to his disciples, and the disciples to the multitude.

Matthew 14:19

ANSWER

And they did all eat, and were filled: and they took up of the fragments that remained twelve baskets full.

And they that had eaten were about five thousand men, beside women and children.

Matthew 14:20, 21

PRAYER: Healing of blind man
And, behold, two blind men sitting by the way
side, when they heard that Jesus passed by, cried
out, saying, Have mercy on us, O Lord, thou son
of David.

Matthew 20:30

ANSWER
So Jesus had compassion on them, and
touched their eyes: and immediately their eyes
received sight, and they followed him.

Matthew 20:34

PRAYER: Jesus prays for a submissive will
And he went a little farther, and fell on his
face, and prayed, saying, O my Father, if it be
possible, let this cup pass from me: nevertheless
not as I will, but as thou wilt.

Matthew 26:39

ANSWER
Who in the days of his flesh, when he had
offered up prayers and supplications with strong
crying and tears unto him that was able to save
him from death, and was heard in that he feared;

Hebrews 5:7

PRAYER: Healing of a paralytic

And they come unto him, bringing one sick of the palsy, which was borne of four.

And when they could not come nigh unto him for the press, they uncovered the roof where he was: and when they had broken it up, they let down the bed wherein the sick of the palsy lay.

When Jesus saw their faith, he said unto the sick of the palsy, Son, thy sins be forgiven thee.

Mark 2:3-5

ANSWER

And immediately he arose, took up the bed, and went forth before them all; insomuch that they were all amazed, and glorified God, saying, We never saw it on this fashion.

Mark 2:12

PRAYER: Peter walks on the water

But when he saw the wind boisterous, he was afraid; and beginning to sink, he cried, saying, Lord, save me.

Matthew 14:30

ANSWER

And immediately Jesus stretched forth his hand, and caught him, and said unto him, O thou of little faith, wherefore didst thou doubt?

And when they were come into the ship, the wind ceased.

Matthew 14:31, 32

PRAYER: Deliverance of Canaanite woman's daughter

And, behold, a woman of Canaan came out of the same coasts, and cried unto him, saying, Have mercy on me, O Lord, thou son of David; my daughter is grievously vexed with a devil.

Matthew 15:22

ANSWER

Then Jesus answered and said unto her, O woman, great is thy faith: be it unto thee even as thou wilt. And her daughter was made whole from that very hour.

Matthew 15:28

PRAYER: Healing of epileptic son

Lord, have mercy on my son: for he is lunatic, and sore vexed: for ofttimes he falleth into the fire, and oft into the water.

Matthew 17:15

ANSWER

And Jesus rebuked the devil; and he departed out of him: and the child was cured from that very hour.

Matthew 17:18

PRAYER: Healing of centurion's servant

Wherefore neither thought I myself worthy to come unto thee: but say in a word, and my servant shall be healed.

For I also am a man set under authority, having under me soldiers, and I say unto one, Go, and he goeth; and to another, Come, and he cometh; and to my servant, Do this, and he doeth it.

Luke 7:7, 8

ANSWER

When Jesus heard these things, he marvelled at him, and turned him about, and said unto the people that followed him, I say unto you, I have not found so great faith, no, not in Israel.

And they that were sent, returning to the house, found the servant whole that had been sick.

Luke 7:9, 10

PRAYER: Cleansing of lepers

And as he entered into a certain village, there met him ten men that were lepers, which stood afar off:

And they lifted up their voices, and said, Jesus, Master, have mercy on us.

Luke 17:12, 13

ANSWER

And one of them, when he saw that he was healed, turned back, and with a loud voice glorified God,

Luke 17:15

PRAYER: Healing of nobleman's son

When he heard that Jesus was come out of Judea into Galilee, he went unto him, and besought him that he would come down, and heal his son: for he was at the point of death.

John 4:47

ANSWER

Then inquired he of them the hour when he began to amend. And they said unto him, Yesterday at the seventh hour the fever left him.

So the father knew that it was at the same hour, in the which Jesus said unto him, Thy son liveth: and himself believed, and his whole house.

John 4:52, 53

PRAYER: Lazarus raised from dead

Then they took away the stone from the place where the dead was laid. And Jesus lifted up his eyes, and said, Father, I thank thee that thou hast heard me.

And I knew that thou hearest me always: but because of the people which stand by I said it, that they may believe that thou hast sent me.

And when he thus had spoken, he cried with a loud voice, Lazarus, come forth.

John 11:41-43

ANSWER

And he that was dead came forth, bound hand and foot with graveclothes: and his face was bound

about with a napkin. Jesus saith unto them, Loose
him, and let him go.

John 11:44

PRAYER: Of penitent thief
And he said unto Jesus, Lord, remember me
when thou comest into thy kingdom.

Luke 23:42

ANSWER
And Jesus said unto him, Verily I say unto
thee, Today shalt thou be with me in paradise.

Luke 23:43

PRAYER: The raising of Dorcas.
Then Peter arose and went with them. When
he was come, they brought him into the upper
chamber: and all the widows stood by him weeping, and shewing the coats and garments which
Dorcas made, while she was with them.

Acts 9:39

ANSWER
And he gave her his hand, and lifted her up,
and when he had called the saints and widows,
presented her alive.

Acts 9:41

PRAYER: Healing of lame man at Gate Beautiful

Then Peter said, Silver and gold have I none; but such as I have give I thee: In the name of Jesus Christ of Nazareth rise up and walk.

Acts 3:6

ANSWER

And he leaping up stood, and walked, and entered with them into the temple, walking, and leaping, and praising God.

Acts 3:8

PRAYER: Peter released from prison

Peter therefore was kept in prison: but prayer was made without ceasing of the church unto God for him.

Acts 12:5

ANSWER

And when Peter was come to himself, he said, Now I know of a surety, that the Lord hath sent his angel, and hath delivered me out of the hand of Herod, and from all the expectation of the people of the Jews.

Acts 12:11

PRAYER: Paul prays for Publius' father

And it came to pass, that the father of Publius lay sick of a fever and of a bloody flux: to whom Paul entered in, and prayed, and laid his hands on him, and healed him.

Acts 28:8

ANSWER

So when this was done, others also, which had diseases in the island, came, and were healed:

Acts 28:9

PRAYER: Paul and Silas released from jail

And at midnight Paul and Silas prayed, and sang praises unto God: and the prisoners heard them.

Acts 16:25

ANSWER

And suddenly there was a great earthquake, so that the foundations of the prison were shaken: and immediately all the doors were opened, and everyone's bands were loosed.

Acts 16:26

PRAYER: The safety of the shipwrecked

For there stood by me this night the angel of God, whose I am, and whom I serve,

Saying, Fear not, Paul; thou must be brought before Caesar: and, lo, God hath given thee all them that sail with thee.

Wherefore, sirs, be of good cheer; for I believe God, that it shall be even as it was told me.

Acts 27:23-25

ANSWER

And the rest, some on boards, and some on broken pieces of the ship. And so it came to pass, that they escaped all safe to land.

Acts 27:44

Intercessory Prayer

Jesus' Intercession for Us

By so much was Jesus made a surety of a better treatment.

Wherefore he is able also to save them to the uttermost that come unto God by him, seeing he ever liveth to make intercession for them.

Hebrews 7:22, 25

And the Lord said, Simon, Simon, behold, Satan hath desired to have you, that he may sift you as wheat:

But I have prayed for thee, that thy faith fail not: and when thou art converted, strengthen thy brethren.

Luke 22:31-32

At that day ye shall ask in my name: and I say not unto you, that I will pray the Father for you:

John 16:26

I pray for them: I pray not for the world, but for them which thou hast given me; for they are thine.

I pray not that thou shouldest take them out of the world, but that thou shouldest keep them from the evil.

Neither pray I for these alone, but for them also which shall believe on me through their word;

John 17:9, 15, 20

And he that searcheth the hearts knoweth what is the mind of the Spirit, because he maketh intercession for the saints according to the will of God.

Romans 8:27

It is Christ that died, yea rather, that is risen again, who is even at the right hand of God, who also maketh intercession for us.

Romans 8:34b

And when he was come near, he beheld the city, and wept over it,

Luke 19:41

When Jesus therefore saw her weeping, and the Jews also weeping which came with her, he groaned in the spirit, and was troubled,

And said, Where have ye laid him? They said unto him, Lord, come and see.

Jesus wept.

Then said the Jews, Behold how he loved him!

John 11:33-36

Who in the days of his flesh, when he had offered up prayers and supplications with strong crying and tears unto him that was able to save him from death, and was heard in that he feared;

Hebrews 5:7

Our Intercession for Others

And the Lord said, Because the cry of Sodom and Gomorrah is great, and because their sin is very grievous;

I will go down now, and see whether they have altogether according to the cry of it, which is come unto me; and if not, I will know.

And the men turned their faces from thence, and went toward Sodom: but Abraham stood yet before the Lord.

And Abraham drew near, and said, Wilt thou also destroy the righteous with the wicked?

Peradventure there be fifty righteous within the city: wilt thou also destroy and not spare the place for the fifty righteous that are therein?

That be far from thee to do after this manner, to slay the righteous with the wicked: and that the righteous should be as the wicked, that be far from thee: Shall not the Judge of all the earth do right?

And the Lord said, If I find in Sodom fifty righteous within the city, then I will spare all the place for their sakes.

And Abraham answered and said, Behold now, I have taken upon me to speak unto the Lord, which am but dust and ashes:

Peradventure there shall lack five of the fifty righteous: wilt thou destroy all the city for lack of five? And he said, If I find there forty and five, I will not destroy it.

And he spake unto him yet again, and said, Peradventure there shall be forty found there. And he said, I will not do it for forty's sake.

And he said unto him, Oh let not the Lord be angry, and I will speak: Peradventure there shall thirty be found there. And he said, I will not do it, if I find thirty there.

And he said, Behold now, I have taken upon me to speak unto the Lord: Peradventure there shall be twenty found there. And he said, I will not destroy it for twenty's sake.

And he said, Oh let not the Lord be angry, and I will speak yet but this once: Peradventure ten shall be found there. And he said, I will not destroy it for ten's sake.

And the Lord went his way, as soon as he had left communing with Abraham: and Abraham returned unto his place.

Genesis 18:20-33

And the Lord was very angry with Aaron to have destroyed him: and I prayed for Aaron also the same time.

I prayed therefore unto the Lord, and said, O Lord God, destroy not thy people and thine inheritance, which thou hast redeemed through thy greatness, which thou hast brought forth out of Egypt with a mighty hand.

Deuteronomy 9:20, 26

And Samuel said, Gather all Israel to Mizpeh, and I will pray for you unto the Lord.

And the children of Israel said to Samuel, Cease not to cry unto the Lord our God for us, that he will save us out of the hand of the Philistines.

I Samuel 7:5, 8

If my people, which are called by my name, shall humble themselves, and pray, and seek my face, and turn from their wicked ways; then will I hear from heaven, and will forgive their sin, and will heal their land.

II Chronicles 7:14

And he saw that there was no man, and wondered that there was no intercessor: therefore his arm brought salvation unto him; and his righteousness, it sustained him.

Isaiah 59:16

I have set watchmen upon thy walls, O Jerusalem, which shall never hold their peace day nor night: ye that make mention of the Lord, keep not silence,

Isaiah 62:6

And there is none that calleth upon thy name, that stirreth up himself to take hold of thee: for thou hast hid thy face from us, and hast consumed us, because of our iniquities.

Isaiah 64:7

Who hath heard such a thing? who hath seen such things? Shall the earth be made to bring forth in one day? or shall a nation be born at once? for as soon as Zion travailed, she brought forth her children.

Isaiah 66:8

And it was so, that after the Lord had spoken these words unto Job, the Lord said to Eliphaz the Temanite, My wrath is kindled against thee, and against thy two friends: for ye have not spoken of me the thing that is right, as my servant Job hath.

Therefore take unto you now seven bullocks and seven rams, and go to my servant Job, and offer up for yourselves a burnt offering; and my servant Job shall pray for you: for him will I accept: lest I deal with you after your folly, in that ye have not spoken of me the thing which is right, like my servant Job.

So Eliphaz the Temanite and Bildad the Shuhite and Zophar the Naamathite went, and did according as the Lord commanded them: the Lord also accepted Job.

And the Lord turned the captivity of Job, when he prayed for his friends: also the Lord gave Job twice as much as he had before.

Job 42:7-10

And I sought for a man among them, that should make up the hedge, and stand in the gap before me for the land, that I should not destroy it: but I found none.

Ezekiel 22:30

And I set my face unto the Lord God, to seek by prayer and supplications, with fasting, and sackcloth, and ashes:

And I prayed unto the Lord my God, and made my confession, and said, O Lord, the great and dreadful God, keeping the covenant and mercy to them that love him, and to them that keep his commandments;

Daniel 9:3, 4

And shall not God avenge his own elect, which cry day and night unto him, though he bear long with them.

Luke 18:7

I have seen, I have seen the affliction of my people which is in Egypt, and I have heard their groaning, and am come down to deliver them. And now come, I will send thee into Egypt.

Acts 7:34

Brethren, my heart's desire and prayer to God for Israel is, that they might be saved.

Romans 10:1

Now I beseech you, brethren, for the Lord Jesus Christ's sake, and for the love of the Spirit, that ye strive together with me in your prayers to God for me;

Romans 15:30

Ye also helping together by prayer for us, that for the gift bestowed upon us by the means of many persons thanks may be given by many on our behalf.

II Corinthians 1:11

Cease not to give thanks for you, making mention of you in my prayers;

Ephesians 1:16

Praying always with all prayer and supplication in the Spirit, and watching thereunto with all perseverance and supplication for all saints;

And for me, that utterance may be given unto me, that I may open my mouth boldly, to make known the mystery of the gospel,

Ephesians 6:18, 19

I thank my God upon every remembrance of you,

Always in every prayer of mine for you all making request with joy,

For your fellowship in the gospel from the first day until now;

Being confident of this very thing, that he which hath begun a good work in you will perform it until the day of Jesus Christ:

Philippians 1:3-6

For this cause we also, since the day we heard it, do not cease to pray for you, and to desire that ye might be filled with the knowledge of his will in all wisdom and spiritual understanding;

That ye might walk worthy of the Lord unto all pleasing, being fruitful in every good work, and increasing in the knowledge of God;

Strengthened with all might, according to his glorious power, unto all patience and longsuffering with joyfulness;

Giving thanks unto the Father, which hath made us meet to be partakers of the inheritance of the saints in light:

Who hath delivered us from the power of darkness, and hath translated us into the kingdom of his dear Son:

Colossians 1:9-13

For what thanks can we render to God again for you, for all the joy wherewith we joy for your sakes before our God;

Night and day praying exceedingly that we might see your face, and might perfect that which is lacking in your faith?

Now God himself and our Father, and our Lord Jesus Christ, direct our way unto you.

And the Lord make you to increase and abound in love one toward another, and toward all men, even as we do toward you:

To the end he may stablish your hearts unblameable in holiness before God, even our Father, at the coming of our Lord Jesus Christ with all his saints.

I Thessalonians 3:9-13

Wherefore also we pray always for you, that our God would count you worthy of this calling, and fulfil all the good pleasure of his goodness, and the work of faith with power:

II Thessalonians 1:11

FINALLY, brethren, pray for us, that the word of the Lord may have free course, and be glorified, even as it is with you:

And that we may be delivered from unreasonable and wicked men: for all men have not faith.

But the Lord is faithful, who shall stablish you, and keep you from evil.

And we have confidence in the Lord touching you, that ye both do and will do the things which we command you.

And the Lord direct your hearts into the love of God, and into the patient waiting for Christ.

II Thessalonians 3:1-5

I exhort therefore, that, first of all, supplications, prayers, intercessions, and giving of thanks, be made for all men;

For kings, and for all that are in authority; that we may lead a quiet and peaceable life in all godliness and honesty.

I Timothy 2:1, 2

But withal prepare me also a lodging: for I trust that through your prayers I shall be given unto you.

Philemon 22

And this is the confidence that we have in him, that, if we ask any thing according to his will, he heareth us:

And if we know that he hear us, whatsoever we ask, we know that we have the petitions that we desired of him.

If any man see his brother sin a sin which is not unto death, he shall ask, and he shall give him life for them that sin not unto death. There is a sin unto death: I do not say that he shall pray for it.

I John 5:14-16

Then said his servants unto him, What thing is this that thou hast done? thou didst fast and weep for the child, while it was alive; but when the child was dead, thou didst rise and eat bread.

And he said, While the child was yet alive, I fasted and wept: for I said, Who can tell whether God will be gracious to me, that the child may live?

II Samuel 12:21, 22

Turn again, and tell Hezekiah the captain of my people, Thus saith the Lord, the God of David thy father, I have heard thy prayer, I have seen thy tears: behold, I will heal thee: on the third day thou shalt go up unto the house of the Lord.

II Kings 20:5

The Holy Spirit in Intercession

If ye then, being evil, know how to give good gifts unto your children: how much more shall your heavenly Father give the Holy Spirit to them that ask him?

Luke 11:13

And, behold, I send the promise of my Father upon you: but tarry ye in the city of Jerusalem, until ye be endued with power from on high.

Luke 24:49

But the Comforter, which is the Holy Ghost, whom the Father will send in my name, he shall teach you all things, and bring all things to your remembrance, whatsoever I have said unto you.

John 14:26

But when the Comforter is come, whom I will send unto you from the Father, even the Spirit of truth, which proceedeth from the Father, he shall testify of me:

John 15:26

And when the day of Pentecost was fully come, they were all with one accord in one place.

And suddenly there came a sound from heaven as of a rushing mighty wind, and it filled all the house where they were sitting.

And there appeared unto them cloven tongues like as of fire, and it sat upon each of them.

And they were all filled with the Holy Ghost, and began to speak with other tongues, as the Spirit gave them utterance.

Acts 2:1-4

For he that speaketh in an unknown tongue speaketh not unto men, but unto God: for no man understandeth him; howbeit in the spirit he speaketh mysteries.

But he that prophesieth speaketh unto men to edification, and exhortation, and comfort.

He that speaketh in an unknown tongue edifieth himself; but he that prophesieth edifieth the church.

For if I pray in an unknown tongue, my spirit prayeth, but my understanding is unfruitful.

What is it then? I will pray with the spirit, and I will pray with the understanding also: I will sing with the spirit, and I will sing with the understanding also.

I Corinthians 14:2-4, 14-15

And, being assembled together with them, commanded them that they should not depart from Jerusalem, but wait for the promise of the Father, which, saith he, ye have heard of me.

For John truly baptized with water; but ye shall be baptized with the Holy Ghost not many days hence.

Acts 1:4, 5

Likewise the Spirit also helpeth our infirmities: for we know not what we should pray for as we ought: but the Spirit itself maketh intercession for us with groanings which cannot be uttered.

Romans 8:26

Praying always with all prayer and supplication in the Spirit, and watching thereunto with all perseverance and supplication for all saints;

Ephesians 6:18

Continue in prayer, and watch in the same with thanksgiving;

Colossians 4:2

But ye, beloved, building up yourselves on your most holy faith, praying in the Holy Ghost,

Keep yourselves in the love of God, looking for the mercy of our Lord Jesus Christ unto eternal life.

Jude 20,21

Howbeit when he, the Spirit of truth, is come, he will guide you into all truth: for he shall not speak of himself; but whatsoever he shall hear, that shall he speak; and he will show you things to come.

John 16:13

Then laid they their hands on them, and they received the Holy Ghost.

Acts 8:17

And when Paul had laid his hands upon them, the Holy Ghost came on them; and they spake with tongues, and prophesied.

Acts 19:6

Great Intercessors…

Jesus Christ

And, behold, there was a man in Jerusalem, whose name was Simeon; and the same man was just and devout, waiting for the consolation of Israel: and the Holy Ghost was upon him.

And it was revealed unto him by the Holy Ghost, that he should not see death, before he had seen the Lord's Christ.

And he came by the Spirit into the temple: and when the parents brought in the child Jesus, to do for him after the custom of the law,

Then took he him up in his arms, and blessed God, and said,

Lord, now lettest thou thy servant depart in peace, according to thy word:

For mine eyes have seen thy salvation,

And Simeon blessed them, and said unto Mary his mother, Behold, this child is set for the fall and rising again of many in Israel; and for a sign which shall be spoken against;

Luke 2:25-30, 34

DEDICATION

Now when all the people were baptized, it came to pass, that Jesus also being baptized, and praying, the heaven was opened,

And the Holy Ghost descended in a bodily shape like a dove upon him, and a voice came from heaven, which said, Thou art my beloved Son; in thee I am well pleased.

Luke 3:21, 22

SEPARATION

But so much the more went there a fame abroad of him: and great multitudes came together to hear, and to be healed by him of their infirmities.

And he withdrew himself into the wilderness, and prayed.

Luke 5:15, 16

DIRECTION

And it came to pass in those days, that he went out into a mountain to pray, and continued all night in prayer to God.

And when it was day, he called unto him his disciples: and of them he chose twelve, whom also he named apostles;

Simon, (whom he also named Peter,) and Andrew his brother, James and John, Philip and Bartholomew,

Matthew and Thomas, James the son of Alphaeus, and Simon called Zelotes,

And Judas the brother of James, and Judas Iscariot, which also was the traitor.

Luke 6:12-16

REVELATION

And it came to pass, as he was alone praying, his disciples were with him: and he asked them, saying, Whom say the people that I am?

They answering said, John the Baptist; but some say, Elias; and others say, that one of the old prophets is risen again.

He said unto them, But whom say ye that I am? Peter answering said, The Christ of God.

Luke 9:18-20

GLORIFICATION

And as he prayed, the fashion of his countenance was altered, and his raiment was white and glistering.

Luke 9:29

These words spake Jesus, and lifted up his eyes to heaven, and said, Father, the hour is come; glorify thy Son, that thy Son also may glorify thee:

As thou hast given him power over all flesh, that he should give eternal life to as many as thou hast given him.

And this is life eternal, that they might know thee the only true God, and Jesus Christ, whom thou hast sent.

I have glorified thee on the earth: I have finished the work which thou gavest me to do.

And now, O Father, glorify thou me with thine own self with the glory which I had with thee before the world was.

I have manifested thy name unto the men which thou gavest me out of the world: thine they were, and thou gavest them me; and they have kept thy word.

Now they have known that all things whatsoever thou hast given me are of thee.

For I have given unto them the words which thou gavest me: and they have received them, and have known surely that I came out from thee, and they have believed that thou didst send me.

I pray for them: I pray not for the world, but for them which thou hast given me: for they are thine.

And all mine are thine, and thine are mine: and I am glorified in them.

John 17:1-10

OBEDIENCE

And he came out, and went, as he was wont, to the mount of Olives; and his disciples also followed him.

And when he was at the place, he said unto them, Pray that ye enter not into temptation.

And he was withdrawn from them about a stone's cast, and kneeled down, and prayed,

Saying, Father, if thou be willing, remove this cup from me: nevertheless not my will, but thine, be done.

And there appeared an angel unto him from heaven, strengthening him.

And being in an agony he prayed more earnestly: and his sweat was as it were great drops of blood falling down to the ground.

And when he rose up from prayer, and was come to his disciples, he found them sleeping for sorrow,

And said unto them, Why sleep ye? rise and pray, lest ye enter into temptation.

Luke 22:39-46

REDEMPTION

And the Redeemer shall come to Zion, and unto them that turn from transgression in Jacob, saith the LORD.

As for me, this is my covenant with them, saith the LORD: My spirit that is upon thee, and my words which I have put in thy mouth, shall not depart out of thy mouth, nor out of the mouth of thy seed, nor out of the mouth of thy seed's seed, saith the LORD, from henceforth and for ever.

Isaiah 59:20-21

PERSECUTORS

But the chief priests and elders persuaded the multitude that they should ask Barabbas, and destroy Jesus.

The governor answered and said unto them, Whether of the twain will ye that I release unto you? They said, Barabbas.

Pilate saith unto them, What shall I do then with Jesus which is called Christ? They all say unto him, Let him be crucified.

And they stripped him, and put on him a scarlet robe.

And when they had platted a crown of thorns, they put it upon his head, and a reed in his right hand: and they bowed the knee before him, and mocked him, saying, Hail, King of the Jews!

And they spit upon him, and took the reed, and smote him on the head.

And after that they had mocked him, they took the robe off from him, and put his own raiment on him, and led him away to crucify him.

Matthew 27:20-22, 28-31

PROPHECY

My God, my God, why hast thou forsaken me? why art thou so far from helping me, and from the words of my roaring?

I am poured out like water, and all my bones are out of joint: my heart is like wax; it is melted in the midst of my bowels.

My strength is dried up like a potsherd; and my tongue cleaveth to my jaws; and thou hast brought me into the dust of death.

For dogs have compassed me: the assembly of the wicked have enclosed me: they pierced my hands and my feet.

I may tell all my bones: they look and stare upon me.

They part my garments among them, and cast lots upon my vesture.

Psalm 22:1, 14-18

PRESENTATION

And when Jesus had cried with a loud voice, he said, Father, into thy hands I commend my spirit: and having said thus, he gave up the ghost.

Luke 23:46

But Christ being come an high priest of good things to come, by a greater and more perfect tabernacle, not made with hands, that is to say, not of this building;

Neither by the blood of goats and calves, but by his own blood he entered in once into the holy place, having obtained eternal redemption for us.

And for this cause he is the mediator of the new testament, that by means of death, for the redemption of the transgressions that were under the first testament, they which are called might receive the promise of eternal inheritance.

Hebrews 9:11-12, 15

Paul

BEHOLD, HE PRAYETH

And the Lord said unto him, Arise, and go into the street which is called Straight, and inquire in the house of Judas for one called Saul, of Tarsus: for, behold, he prayeth.

Acts 9:11

POWER AND KNOWLEDGE

Wherefore I also, after I heard of your faith in the Lord Jesus, and love unto all the saints,

Cease not to give thanks for you, making mention of you in my prayers;

That the God of our Lord Jesus Christ, the Father of glory, may give unto you the spirit of wisdom and revelation in the knowledge of him:

The eyes of your understanding being enlightened; that ye may know what is the hope of his calling, and what the riches of the glory of his inheritance in the saints,

And what is the exceeding greatness of his power to us-ward who believe, according to the working of his mighty power,

Which he wrought in Christ, when he raised him from the dead, and set him at his own right hand in the heavenly places,

For above all principality, and power, and might, and dominion, and every name that is named, not only in this world, but also in that which is to come.

Ephesians 1:15-21

PERSONAL PENTECOST

Wherefore I desire that ye faint not at my tribulations for you, which is your glory.

For this cause I bow my knees unto the Father of our Lord Jesus Christ,

Of whom the whole family in heaven and earth is named,

That he would grant you, according to the riches of his glory, to be strengthened with might by his Spirit in the inner man;

That Christ may dwell in your hearts by faith; that ye, being rooted and grounded in love,

May be able to comprehend with all saints what is the breadth, and length, and depth, and height;

And to know the love of Christ, which passeth knowledge, that ye might be filled with all the fulness of God.

Now unto him that is able to do exceeding abundantly above all that we ask or think, according to the power that worketh in us,

Unto him be glory in the church by Christ Jesus throughout all ages, world without end. Amen.

Ephesians 3:13-21

PERSEVERANCE

And this I pray, that your love may abound yet more and more in knowledge and in all judgment;

That ye may approve things that are excellent; that ye may be sincere and without offence till the day of Christ;

Being filled with the fruits of righteousness, which are by Jesus Christ, unto the glory and praise of God.

Philippians 1:9-11

PERCEPTION

For this cause we also, since the day we heard it, do not cease to pray for you, and to desire that ye might be filled with the knowledge of his will in all wisdom and spiritual understanding;

That ye might walk worthy of the Lord unto all pleasing, being fruitful in every good work, and increasing in the knowledge of God;

Strengthened with all might, according to his glorious power, unto all patience and longsuffering with joyfulness;

Giving thanks unto the Father, which hath made us meet to be partakers of the inheritance of the saints in light:

Who hath delivered us from the power of darkness, and hath translated us into the kingdom of his dear Son:

Colossians 1:9-13

PERFECTION

For what thanks can we render to God again for you, for all the joy wherewith we joy for your sakes before our God;

Night and day praying exceedingly that we might see your face, and might perfect that which is lacking in your faith?

Now God himself and our Father, and our Lord Jesus Christ, direct our way unto you.

And the Lord make you to increase and abound in love one toward another, and toward all men, even as we do toward you:

To the end he may stablish your hearts unblameable in holiness before God, even our Father, at the coming of our Lord Jesus Christ with all his saints.

I Thessalonians 3:9-13

PAIN

And lest I should be exalted above measure through the abundance of the revelations, there was given to me a thorn in the flesh, the messenger of Satan to buffet me, lest I should be exalted above measure.

For this thing I besought the Lord thrice, that it might depart from me.

And he said unto me, My grace is sufficient for thee: for my strength is made perfect in weakness. Most gladly therefore will I rather glory in my infirmities, that the power of Christ may rest upon me.

II Corinthians 12:7-9

PERSECUTION

And at midnight Paul and Silas prayed, and

sang praises unto God: and the prisoners heard them.

And suddenly there was a great earthquake, so that the foundations of the prison were shaken: and immediately all the doors were opened, and every one's bands were loosed.

Acts 16:25, 26

PRESSURES

Finally, brethren, pray for us, that the word of the Lord may have free course, and be glorified, even as it is with you:

And that we may be delivered from unreasonable and wicked men: for all men have not faith.

II Thessalonians 3:1, 2

PEACE

Now the Lord of peace himself give you peace always by all means. The Lord be with you all.

II Thessalonians 3:16

PLEASING LIFE

Now the God of peace, that brought again from the dead our Lord Jesus, that great shepherd of the sheep, through the blood of the everlasting covenant,

Make you perfect in every good work to do his will, working in you that which is well-pleasing in his sight, through Jesus Christ; to whom be glory for ever and ever. Amen.

Hebrews 13:20, 21

PRESERVED

And the very God of peace sanctify you wholly; and I pray God your whole spirit and soul and body be preserved blameless unto the coming of our Lord Jesus Christ.

I Thessalonians 5:23

PLEASURE

Wherefore also we pray always for you, that our God would count you worthy of this calling, and fulfil all the good pleasure of his goodness, and the work of faith with power:

That the name of our Lord Jesus Christ may be glorified in you, and ye in him, according to the grace of our God and the Lord Jesus Christ.

II Thessalonians 1:11, 12

PERMANENCY

Pray without ceasing.

In every thing give thanks: for this is the will of God in Christ Jesus concerning you.

And the very God of peace sanctify you wholly; and I pray God your whole spirit and soul and body be preserved blameless unto the coming of our Lord Jesus Christ.

Faithful is he that calleth you, who also will do it.

Brethren, pray for us.

I Thessalonians 5:17-18, 23-25

Jehosaphat

So the king of Israel and Jehoshaphat the king of Judah went up to Ramothgilead.

And the king of Israel said unto Jehoshaphat, I will disguise myself, and will go to the battle.

Now the king of Syria had commanded the captains of the chariots that were with him, saying, Fight ye not with small or great, save only with the king of Israel.

And it came to pass, when the captains of the chariots saw Jehoshaphat, that they said, It is the king of Israel. Therefore they compassed about him to fight: but Jehoshaphat cried out, and the LORD helped him; and God moved them to depart from him.

II Chronicles 18:28-31

And Jehoshaphat stood in the congregation of Judah and Jerusalem, in the house of the Lord, before the new court.

And said, O Lord God of our fathers, art not thou God in heaven? and rulest not thou over all the kingdoms of the heathen? and in thine hand is there not power and might, so that none is able to withstand thee?

Art not thou our God, who didst drive out the inhabitants of this land before thy people Israel, and gavest it to the seed of Abraham thy friend for ever?

And they dwelt therein, and have built thee a sanctuary therein for thy name, saying,

If, when evil cometh upon us, as the sword, judgment, or pestilence, or famine, we stand before this house, and in thy presence, (for thy name is in this house,) and cry unto thee in our affliction, then thou wilt hear and help.

II Chronicles 20:5-9

Ezra

Then I proclaimed a fast there, at the river of Ahava, that we might afflict ourselves before our God, to seek of him a right way for us, and for our little ones and for all our substance.

For I was ashamed to require of the king a band of soldiers and horsemen to help us against the enemy in the way: because we had spoken unto the king, saying, The hand of our God is upon all them for good that seek him; but his power and his wrath is against all them that forsake him.

So we fasted and besought our God for this: and he was entreated of us.

Ezra 8:21-23

Zacharias

And the whole multitude of the people were praying without at the time of incense.

And there appeared unto him an angel of the Lord standing on the right side of the altar of incense.

And when Zacharias saw him, he was troubled, and fear fell upon him.

But the angel said unto him, Fear not, Zacharias: for thy prayer is heard; and thy wife Elisabeth shall bear thee a son, and thou shalt call his name John.

Luke 1:10-13

Hezekiah

Go, and say to Hezekiah, Thus saith the Lord, the God of David thy father, I have heard thy prayer, I have seen thy tears: behold, I will add unto thy days fifteen years.

And I will deliver thee and this city out of the hand of the king of Assyria: and I will defend this city.

And this shall be a sign unto thee from the Lord, that the Lord will do this thing that he hath spoken;

Behold, I will bring again the shadow of the degrees, which is gone down in the sun dial of Ahaz, ten degrees backward. So the sun returned ten degrees, by which degrees it was gone down.

The writing of Hezekiah king of Judah, when he had been sick, and was recovered of his sickness:

Isaiah 38:5-9

Jeremiah

Blessed is the man that trusteth in the Lord, and whose hope the Lord is.

For he shall be as a tree planted by the waters, and that spreadeth out her roots by the river, and shall not see when heat cometh, but her leaf shall be green; and shall not be careful in the year of drought, neither shall cease from yielding fruit.

The heart is deceitful above all things, and desperately wicked: who can know it?

I the Lord search the heart, I try the reins, even to give every man according to his ways, and according to the fruit of his doings.

As the partridge sitteth on eggs, and hatcheth them not; so he that getteth riches, and not by right, shall leave them in the midst of his days, and at his end shall be a fool.

A glorious high throne from the beginning is the place of our sanctuary.

O Lord, the hope of Israel, all that forsake thee shall be ashamed, and they that depart from me shall be written in the earth, because they have forsaken the Lord, the fountain of living waters.

Heal me, O Lord, and I shall be healed; save me, and I shall be saved: for thou art my praise.

Behold, they say unto me, Where is the word of the Lord? let it come now.

As for me, I have not hastened from being a pastor to follow thee: neither have I desired the woeful day; thou knowest: that which came out of my lips was right before me.

Be not a terror unto me: thou art my hope in the day of evil.

Let them be confounded that persecute me, but let not me be confounded: let them be dismayed, but let not me be dismayed: bring upon them the day of evil, and destroy them with double destruction.

Jeremiah 17:7-18

Moses

I prayed therefore unto the LORD, and said, O Lord GOD, destroy not thy people and thine inheritance, which thou hast redeemed through thy greatness, which thou hast brought forth out of Egypt with a mighty hand.

Remember thy servants, Abraham, Isaac, and Jacob; look not unto the stubbornness of this people, nor to their wickedness, nor to their sin:

Lest the land whence thou broughtest us out say, Because the LORD was not able to bring them into the land which he promised them, and because he hated them, he hath brought them out to slay them in the wilderness.

Yet they are thy people and thine inheritance, which thou broughtest out by thy mighty power and by thy stretched out arm.

Deuteronomy 9:26-29

Jacob

Deliver me, I pray thee, from the hand of my brother, from the hand of Esau: for I fear him, lest he will come and smite me, and the mother with the children.

And thou saidst, I will surely do thee good, and make thy seed as the sand of the sea, which cannot be numbered for multitude.

And he lodged there that same night; and took of that which came to his hand a present for Esau his brother;

Two hundred she goats, and twenty he goats, two hundred ewes, and twenty rams,

Thirty milch camels with their colts, forty kine, and ten bulls, twenty she asses, and ten foals.

And he delivered them into the hand of his servants, every drove by themselves; and said unto his servants, Pass over before me, and put a space betwixt drove and drove.

And he commanded the foremost, saying, When Esau my brother meeteth thee, and asketh thee, saying, Whose art thou? and whither goest thou? and whose are these before thee?

Then thou shalt say, They be thy servant Jacob's; it is a present sent unto my lord Esau: and behold, also he is behind us.

Genesis 32:11-18

Mary

And Mary said, My soul doth magnify the Lord,

And my spirit hath rejoiced in God my Saviour.

For he hath regarded the low estate of his handmaiden: for, behold, from henceforth all generations shall call me blessed.

For he that is mighty hath done to me great things; and holy is his name.

And his mercy is on them that fear him from generation to generation.

He hath shewed strength with his arm; he hath scattered the proud in the imagination of their hearts.

He hath put down the mighty from their seats, and exalted them of low degree.

He hath filled the hungry with good things; and the rich he hath sent empty away.

He hath holpen his servant Israel, in remembrance of his mercy;

As he spake to our fathers, to Abraham, and to his seed for ever.

Luke 1:46-55

Daniel

And in the four and twentieth day of the first month, as I was by the side of the great river, which is Hiddekel;

Then I lifted up mine eyes, and looked, and behold a certain man clothed in linen, whose loins were girded with fine gold of Uphaz:

His body also was like the beryl, and his face as the appearance of lightning, and his eyes as lamps of fire, and his arms and his feet like in colour to polished brass, and the voice of his words like the voice of a multitude.

And I Daniel alone saw the vision: for the men that were with me saw not the vision; but a great quaking fell upon them, so that they fled to hide themselves.

Therefore I was left alone, and saw this great vision, and there remained no strength in me: for my comeliness was turned in me into corruption, and I retained no strength.

Yet heard I the voice of his words: and when I heard the voice of his words, then was I in a deep sleep on my face, and my face toward the ground.

And, behold, an hand touched me, which set me upon my knees and upon the palms of my hands.

And he said unto me, O Daniel, a man greatly beloved, understand the words that I speak unto thee, and stand upright: for unto thee am I now sent. And when he had spoken this word unto me, I stood trembling.

Then said he unto me, Fear not, Daniel: for from the first day that thou didst set thine heart to understand, and to chasten thyself before thy God, thy words were heard, and I am come for thy words.

But the prince of the kingdom of Persia withstood me one and twenty days: but, lo, Michael, one of the chief princes, came to help me: and I remained there with the kings of Persia.

Now I am come to make thee understand what shall befall thy people in the latter days: for yet the vision is many days.

Then said he, Knowest thou wherefore I come unto thee? and now will I return to fight with the princes of Persia: and when I am gone forth, lo, the prince of Grecia shall come.

But I will shew thee that which is noted in the scripture of truth: and there is none that holdeth with me in these things, but Michael your prince.

Daniel 10:4-14, 20-21

Cornelius

And they said, Cornelius the centurion, a just man, and one that feareth God, and of good report among all the nation of the Jews, was warned from God by an holy angel to send for thee into his house, and to hear words of thee.

And the morrow after they entered into Caesarea. And Cornelius waited for them, and had called together his kinsmen and near friends.

Therefore came I unto you without gainsaying, as soon as I was sent for: I ask therefore for what intent ye have sent for me?

And Cornelius said, Four days ago I was fasting until this hour; and at the ninth hour I prayed in my house, and, behold, a man stood before me in bright clothing.

And said, Cornelius, thy prayer is heard, and thine alms are had in remembrance in the sight of God.

Acts 10:22, 24, 29-31

Abraham

And Abraham drew near, and said, Wilt thou also destroy the righteous with the wicked?

Peradventure there be fifty righteous within the city: wilt thou also destroy and not spare the place for the fifty righteous that are therein?

That be far from thee to do after this manner, to slay the righteous with the wicked: and that the righteous should be as the wicked, that be far from thee: Shall not the Judge of all the earth do right?

And the Lord said, If I find in Sodom fifty righteous within the city, then I will spare all the place for their sakes.

And Abraham answered and said, Behold now, I have taken upon me to speak unto the Lord, which am but dust and ashes:

Peradventure there shall lack five of the fifty righteous: wilt thou destroy all the city for lack of five? And he said, If I find there forty and five, I will not destroy it.

And he spake unto him yet again, and said, Peradventure there shall be forty found there. And he said, I will not do it for forty's sake.

And he said unto him, Oh let not the Lord be angry, and I will speak: Peradventure there shall thirty be found there. And he said, I will not do it, if I find thirty there.

And he said, Behold now, I have taken upon me to speak unto the Lord: Peradventure there shall be twenty found there. And he said, I will not destroy it for twenty's sake.

And he said, Oh let not the Lord be angry, and I will speak yet but this once: Peradventure ten shall be found there. And he said, I will not destroy it for ten's sake.

And the LORD went his way, as soon as he had left communing with Abraham: and Abraham returned unto his place.

Genesis 18:23-33

Hosea

Yea, he had power over the angel, and prevailed: he wept, and made supplication unto him: he found him in Bethel, and there he spake with us;

Even the Lord God of hosts; the Lord is his memorial.

Therefore turn thou to thy God: keep mercy and judgment, and wait on thy God continually.

Hosea 12:4-6

Isaac

And Isaac entreated the Lord for his wife, because she was barren: and the Lord was entreated of him, and Rebekah his wife conceived.

Genesis 25:21

Job

And the Lord turned the captivity of Job, when he prayed for his friends: also the Lord gave Job twice as much as he had before.

Job 42:10

Manasseh

And when he was in affliction, he besought the Lord his God, and humbled himself greatly before the God of his fathers,

And prayed unto him: and he was entreated of him, and heard his supplication, and brought him again to Jerusalem into his kingdom. Then Manasseh knew that the Lord he was God.

II Chronicles 33:12, 13

Hannah

And she said, Oh my lord, as thy soul liveth, my lord, I am the woman that stood by thee here, praying unto the Lord.

For this child I prayed; and the Lord hath given me my petition which I asked of him:

Therefore also I have lent him to the Lord; as long as he liveth he shall be lent to the Lord. And he worshipped the Lord there.

I Samuel 1:26-28

And Hannah prayed, and said, My heart rejoiceth in the Lord, mine horn is exalted in the Lord: my mouth is enlarged over mine enemies; because I rejoice in thy salvation.

There is none holy as the Lord: for there is

none beside thee: neither is there any rock like our God.

Talk no more so exceeding proudly; let not arrogancy come out of your mouth: for the Lord is a God of knowledge, and by him actions are weighed.

I Samuel 2:1-3

Nehemiah

The words of Nehemiah the son of Hachaliah.

And they said unto me, The remnant that are left of the captivity there in the province are in great affliction and reproach: the wall of Jerusalem also is broken down, and the gates thereof are burned with fire.

And it came to pass, when I heard these words, that I sat down and wept, and mourned certain days, and fasted, and prayed before the God of heaven,

And said, I beseech thee, O Lord God of Heaven, the great and terrible God, that keepeth covenant and mercy for them that love him and observe his commandments:

Let thine ear now be attentive, and thine eyes open, that thou mayest hear the prayer of thy servant, which I pray before thee now, day and night, for the children of Israel thy servants, and confess the sins of the children of Israel, which we have sinned against thee: both I and my father's house have sinned.

We have dealt very corruptly against thee, and have not kept the commandments, nor the judgments, which thou commandedst thy servant Moses.

Remember, I beseech thee, the word that thou commandedst thy servant Moses, saying, If ye transgress, I will scatter you abroad among the nations:

But if ye turn unto me, and keep my commandments, and do them; though there were of you cast out unto the uttermost part of the heaven, yet will I gather them from thence, and will bring them unto the place that I have chosen to set my name there.

Now these are thy servants and thy people, whom thou hast redeemed by thy great power, and by thy strong hand.

O Lord, I beseech thee, let now thine ear be attentive to the prayer of thy servant, and to the prayer of thy servants, who desire to fear thy name: and prosper, I pray thee, thy servant this day, and grant him mercy in the sight of this man. For I was the king's cupbearer.

Nehemiah 1:1a, 3-11

Prayer Promises

Prayer for Others

And for me, that utterance may be given unto me, that I may open my mouth boldly, to make known the mystery of the gospel,

For which I am an ambassador in bonds: that therein I may speak boldly, as I ought to speak.
Ephesians 6:19, 20

Brethren, pray for us.
I Thessalonians 5:25

Finally, brethren, pray for us, that the word of the Lord may have free course, and be glorified, even as it is with you.
II Thessalonians 3:1

Hold fast the form of sound words, which thou hast heard of me, in faith and love which is in Christ Jesus.

That good thing which was committed unto thee keep by the Holy Ghost which dwelleth in us.
II Timothy 1:13, 14

For the eyes of the Lord are over the righteous, and his ears are open unto their prayers: but the face of the Lord is against them that do evil.
I Peter 3:12

When my soul fainted within me I remembered the Lord: and my prayer came in unto thee, into thine holy temple.

Jonah 2:7

And Jesus went into the temple of God, and cast out all them that sold and bought in the temple, and overthrew the tables of the money-changers, and the seats of them that sold doves,

And said unto them, It is written, My house shall be called the house of prayer; but ye have made it a den of thieves.

Matthew 21:12-13

For this cause we also, since the day we heard it, do not cease to pray for you, and to desire that ye might be filled with the knowledge of his will in all wisdom and spiritual understanding;

That ye might walk worthy of the Lord unto all pleasing, being fruitful in every good work, and increasing in the knowledge of God;

Strengthened with all might, according to his glorious power, unto all patience and longsuffering with joyfulness;

Giving thanks unto the Father, which hath made us meet to be partakers of the inheritance of the saints in light:

Who hath delivered us from the power of darkness, and hath translated us into the kingdom of his dear Son:

In whom we have redemption through his blood, even the forgiveness of sins;

Colossians 1:9-14

These all continued with one accord in prayer and supplication, with the women, and Mary the mother of Jesus, and with his brethren.

And they prayed, and said, Thou, Lord, which knowest the hearts of all men, shew whether of these two thou hast chosen,

And they gave forth their lots; and the lot fell upon Mathias; and he was numbered with the eleven apostles.

Acts 1:14, 24, 26

And when they had prayed, the place was shaken where they were assembled together; and they were all filled with the Holy Ghost, and they spake the word of God with boldness.

Acts 4:31

A devout man, and one that feared God with all his house, which gave much alms to the people, and prayed to God alway.

On the morrow, as they went on their journey, and drew nigh unto the city, Peter went up upon the housetop to pray about the sixth hour:

And Cornelius said, Four days ago I was fasting until this hour; and at the ninth hour I prayed in my house, and, behold, a man stood before me in bright clothing,

And said, Cornelius, thy prayer is heard, and thine alms are had in remembrance in the sight of God.

Acts 10:2, 9, 30-31

Peter therefore was kept in prison: but prayer was made without ceasing of the church unto God for him.

Acts 12:5

And when they had fasted and prayed, and laid their hands on them, they sent them away.

Acts 13:3

And when they had ordained them elders in every church, and had prayed with fasting, they commended them to the Lord, on whom they believed.

Acts 14:23

But we will give ourselves continually to prayer, and to the ministry of the word.

Acts 6:4

And there was a certain disciple at Damascus, named Ananias; and to him said the Lord in a vision, Ananias. And he said, Behold, I am here, Lord.

And the Lord said unto him, Arise, and go into the street which is called Straight, and inquire in the house of Judas for one called Saul, of Tarsus: for, behold, he prayeth,

And hath seen in a vision a man named Ananias coming in, and putting his hand on him, that he might receive his sight.

Then Ananias answered, Lord, I have heard by many of this man, how much evil he hath done to thy saints at Jerusalem:

And here he hath authority from the chief priests to bind all that call on thy name.

But the Lord said unto him, Go thy way: for he is a chosen vessel unto me, to bear my name before the Gentiles, and kings, and the children of Israel:

Acts 9:10-15

Wherefore the Lord brought upon them the captains of the host of the king of Assyria, which took Manasseh among the thorns, and bound him with fetters, and carried him to Babylon.

And prayed unto him: and he was entreated of him, and heard his supplication, and brought him again to Jerusalem into his kingdom. Then Manasseh knew that the Lord he was God.

II Chronicles 33:11, 13

Shew us thy mercy, O Lord, and grant us thy salvation.

Psalm 85:7

Behold, the Lord's hand is not shortened, that it cannot save; neither his ear heavy, that it cannot hear;

Isaiah 59:1

And ye shall seek me, and find me, when ye shall search for me with all your heart.

Jeremiah 29:13

And he said unto him, Arise, go thy way: thy faith hath made thee whole.

Luke 17:19

And at midnight Paul and Silas prayed, and sang praises unto God: and the prisoners heard them.

And suddenly there was a great earthquake, so that the foundations of the prison were shaken: and immediately all the doors were opened, and everyone's bands were loosed.

And the keeper of the prison awaking out of his sleep, and seeing the prison doors open, he drew out his sword, and would have killed himself, supposing that the prisoners had been fled.

But Paul cried with a loud voice, saying, Do thyself no harm: for we are all here.

Then he called for a light, and sprang in, and came trembling, and fell down before Paul and Silas,

And brought them out, and said, Sirs, what must I do to be saved?

And they said, Believe on the Lord Jesus Christ, and thou shalt be saved, and thy house.

And they spake unto him the word of the Lord, and to all that were in his house.

And he took them the same hour of the night, and washed their stripes; and was baptized, he and all his, straightway.

And when he had brought them into his house, he set meat before them, and rejoiced, believing in God with all his house.

And when it was day, the magistrates sent the sergeants, saying, Let those men go.

Acts 16:25-35

For what nation is there so great, who hath God so nigh unto them, as the Lord our God is in all things that we call upon him for?

Specially the day that thou stoodest before the Lord thy God in Horeb, when the Lord said unto me, Gather me the people together, and I will make them hear my words, that they may learn to fear me all the days that they shall live upon the earth, and that they may teach their children.

Deuteronomy 4:7, 10

And Samuel said, Gather all Israel to Mizpeh, and I will pray for you unto the Lord.

And they gathered together to Mizpeh, and drew water, and poured it out before the Lord, and fasted on that day, and said there, We have sinned against the Lord. And Samuel judged the children of Israel in Mizpeh.

And Samuel took a sucking lamb, and offered it for a burnt offering wholly unto the Lord: and Samuel cried unto the Lord for Israel; and the Lord heard him.

I Samuel 7:5, 6, 9

That thine eyes may be open toward this house night and day, even toward the place of which thou hast said, My name shall be there: that thou mayest hearken unto the prayer which thy servant shall make toward this place.

If there be in the land famine, if there be pestilence, blasting, mildew, locust, or if there be caterpillar; if their enemy besiege them in the land of their cities; whatsoever plague, whatsoever sickness there be;

What prayer and supplication soever be made by any man, or by all thy people Israel, which shall know every man the plague of his own heart, and spread forth his hands toward this house:

Then hear thou in heaven thy dwelling place, and forgive, and do, and give to every man according to his ways, whose heart thou knowest; (for thou, even thou only, knowest the hearts of all the children of men;)

I Kings 8:29, 37-39

Yet if they shall bethink themselves in the land whither they were carried captives, and repent, and make supplication unto thee in the land of them that carried them captives, saying, We have sinned, and have done perversely, we have committed wickedness;

And so return unto thee with all their heart, and with all their soul, in the land of their enemies, which led them away captive, and pray unto thee toward their land, which thou gavest unto their fathers, the city which thou hast chosen, and the house which I have built for thy name:

Then hear thou their prayer and their supplication in heaven thy dwelling place, and maintain their cause,

And forgive thy people that have sinned against thee, and all their transgressions wherein they have transgressed against thee, and give them compassion before them who carried them captive, that they may have compassion on them:

For they be thy people, and thine inheritance, which thou broughtest forth out of Egypt, from the midst of the furnace of iron:

That thine eyes may be open unto the supplication of thy servant, and unto the supplication of thy people Israel, to hearken unto them in all that they call for unto thee.

For thou didst separate them from among all the people of the earth, to be thine inheritance, as thou spakest by the hand of Moses thy servant, when thou broughtest our fathers out of Egypt, O Lord God.

And it was so, when Solomon had made an end of praying all this prayer and supplication unto the Lord, he arose from before the altar of the Lord, from kneeling on his knees with his hands spread up to heaven.

And he stood, and blessed all the congregation of Israel with a loud voice, saying,

Blessed be the Lord, that hath given rest unto his people Israel, according to all that he promised: there hath not failed one word of all his good promise, which he promised by the hand of Moses his servant.

The Lord our God be with us, as he was with our fathers: let him not leave us, nor forsake us:

That he may incline our hearts unto him, to walk in all his ways, and to keep his commandments, and his statutes, and his judgments, which he commanded our fathers.

And let these my words, wherewith I have made supplication before the Lord, be nigh unto the Lord our God day and night, that he maintain the cause of his servant, and the cause of his people Israel at all times, as the matter shall require:

I Kings 8:47-59

And Asa cried unto the Lord his God, and said, Lord, it is nothing with thee to help, whether with many, or with them that have no power: help us, O Lord our God; for we rest on thee, and in thy name we go against this multitude. O Lord, thou art our God; let not man prevail against thee.

II Chronicles 14:11

And Jehoshaphat stood in the congregation of Judah and Jerusalem, in the house of the Lord, before the new court,

And said, O Lord God of our fathers, art not thou God in heaven? and rulest not thou over all the kingdoms of the heathen? and in thine hand is there not power and might, so that none is able to withstand thee?

Art not thou our God, who didst drive out the inhabitants of this land before thy people Israel, and gavest it to the seed of Abraham thy friend for ever?

And they dwelt therein, and have built thee a sanctuary therein for thy name, saying,

If, when evil cometh upon us, as the sword, judgment, or pestilence, or famine, we stand before this house, and in thy presence, (for thy name is in this house) and cry unto thee in our affliction, then thou wilt hear and help.

And now, behold, the children of Ammon and Moab and mount Seir, whom thou wouldest not let Israel invade, when they came out of the land of Egypt, but they turned from them, and destroyed them not;

Behold, I say, how they reward us, to come to cast us out of thy possession, which thou hast given us to inherit.

O our God, wilt thou not judge them? for we have no might against this great company that cometh against us; neither know we what to do: but our eyes are upon thee.

II Chronicles 20:5-12

When the righteous are in authority, the people rejoice: but when the wicked beareth rule, the people mourn.

Proverbs 29:2

O Lord, though our iniquities testify against us, do thou it for thy name's sake: for our backslidings are many; we have sinned against thee.

We acknowledge, O Lord, our wickedness, and the iniquity of our fathers: for we have sinned against thee.

Jeremiah 14:7, 20

We have sinned, and have commited iniquity, and have done wickedly, and have rebelled, even by departing from thy precepts and from thy judgments:

Neither have we hearkened unto thy servants the prophets, which spake in thy name to our kings, our princes, and our fathers, and to all the people of the land.

O Lord, righteousness belongeth unto thee, but unto us confusion of faces, as at this day; to the men of Judah, and to the inhabitants of Jerusalem, and unto all Israel, that are near, and that are far off, through all the countries whither thou hast driven them, because of their trespass that they have trespassed against thee.

O Lord, to us belongeth confusion of face, to our kings, to our princes, and to our fathers, because we have sinned against thee.

To the Lord our God belong mercies and forgiveness, though we have rebelled against him;

Neither have we obeyed the voice of the Lord our God, to walk in his laws, which he set before us by his servants the prophets.

Yea, all Israel have transgressed thy law, even by departing, that they might not obey thy voice; therefore the curse is poured upon us, and the oath that is written in the law of Moses the servant of God, because we have sinned against him.

And he hath confirmed his words, which he spake against us, and against our judges that judged us, by bringing upon us a great evil: for under the whole heaven hath not been done as hath been done upon Jerusalem.

As it is written in the law of Moses, all this evil is come upon us: yet made we not our prayer before the Lord our God, that we might turn from our iniquities, and understand thy truth.

Therefore hath the Lord watched upon the evil, and brought it upon us: for the Lord our God is righteous in all his works which he doeth: for we obeyed not his voice.

And now, O Lord our God, that hast brought thy people forth out of the land of Egypt with a mighty hand, and hast gotten thee renown, as at this day; we have sinned, we have done wickedly.

Daniel 9:5-15

Brethren, my heart's desire and prayer to God for Israel is, that they might be saved.

Romans 10:1

Prayer for Spiritual Healing

And when Elisha was come into the house, behold, the child was dead, and laid upon his bed.

He went in therefore, and shut the door upon them twain, and prayed unto the Lord.

And he went up, and lay upon the child, and put his mouth upon his mouth, and his eyes upon his eyes, and his hands upon his hands: and he stretched himself upon the child; and the flesh of the child waxed warm.

Then he returned, and walked in the house to and fro; and went up, and stretched himself upon him: and the child sneezed seven times, and the child opened his eyes.

And he called Gehazi, and said, Call this Shunammite. So he called her. And when she was come in unto him, he said, Take up thy son.

Then she went in, and fell at his feet, and bowed herself to the ground, and took up her son, and went out.

II Kings 4:32-37

For there stood by me this night the angel of God, whose I am, and whom I serve,

Saying, Fear not, Paul; thou must be brought before Caesar: and, lo, God hath given thee all them that sail with thee.

Wherefore, sirs, be of good cheer: for I believe God, that it shall be even as it was told me.

Acts 27:23-25

Is any among you afflicted? let him pray. Is any merry? let him sing psalms.

James 5:13

The Lord also will be a refuge for the oppressed, a refuge in times of trouble.

And they that know thy name will put their trust in thee: for thou, Lord, hast not forsaken them that seek thee.

Psalm 9:9-10

For I said in my haste, I am cut off from before thine eyes: nevertheless thou heardest the voice of my supplications when I cried unto thee.

Psalm 31:22

In righteousness shalt thou be established: thou shalt be far from oppression; for thou shalt not fear: and from terror; for it shall not come near thee.

Isaiah 54:14

For I know the thoughts that I think toward you, saith the Lord, thoughts of peace, and not of evil, to give you an expected end.

Then shall ye come upon me, and ye shall go and pray unto me, and I will hearken unto you.

And ye shall seek me, and find me, when ye shall search for me with all your heart.

Jeremiah 29:11-13

Peace I leave with you, my peace I give unto you: not as the world giveth, give I unto you. Let not your heart be troubled, neither let it be afraid.

John 14:27

Grace be to you and peace from God the Father, and from our Lord Jesus Christ,

Who gave himself for our sins, that he might deliver us from this present evil world, according to the will of God and our Father.

Galatians 1:3-4

And be renewed in the spirit of your mind.

Ephesians 4:23

In my distress I called upon the Lord, and cried to my God: and he did hear my voice out of his temple, and my cry did enter into his ears.

II Samuel 22:7

He restoreth my soul: he leadeth me in the paths of righteousness for his name's sake.

Yea, though I walk through the valley of the shadow of death, I will fear no evil: for thou art with me; thy rod and thy staff they comfort me.

Psalm 23:3-4

And Jehoshaphat stood in the congregation of Judah and Jerusalem, in the house of the Lord, before the new court,

And said, O Lord God of our fathers, art not thou God in heaven? and rulest not thou over all the kingdoms of the heathen? and in thine hand is there not power and might, so that none is able to withstand thee?

Art not thou our God, who didst drive out the inhabitants of this land before thy people Israel, and gavest it to the seed of Abraham thy friend for ever?

And they dwelt therein, and have built thee a sanctuary therein for thy name, saying,

If, when evil cometh upon us, as the sword, judgment, or pestilence, or famine, we stand before this house, and in thy presence, (for thy name is in this house) and cry unto thee in our affliction, then thou wilt hear and help.

And now, behold, the children of Ammon and Moab and mount Seir, whom thou wouldest not let Israel invade, when they came out of the land of Egypt, but they turned from them, and destroyed them not;

Behold, I say, how they reward us, to come to cast us out of thy possession, which thou hast given us to inherit.

O our God, wilt thou not judge them? for we have no might against this great company that cometh against us; neither know we what to do: but our eyes are upon thee.

II Chronicles 20:5-12

Therefore thou deliveredst them into the hand of their enemies, who vexed them: and in the time of their trouble, when they cried unto thee, thou heardest them from heaven; and according to thy manifold mercies thou gavest them saviours, who saved them out of the hand of their enemies.

But after they had rest, they did evil again before thee: therefore leftest thou them in the hand of their enemies, so that they had the dominion over them: yet when they returned, and cried unto thee, thou heardest them from heaven; and many times didst thou deliver them according to thy mercies;

Nehemiah 9:27-28

Will God hear his cry when trouble cometh upon him?

Job 27:9

Hear me when I call, O God of my righteousness: thou hast enlarged me when I was in distress; have mercy upon me, and hear my prayer.

Psalm 4:1

In my distress I called upon the Lord, and cried unto my God: he heard my voice out of his temple, and my cry came before him, even into his ears.

Psalm 18:6

My God, my God, why hast thou forsaken me? why art thou so far from helping me, and from the words of my roaring?

Psalm 22:1

They cried unto thee, and were delivered: they trusted in thee, and were not confounded.
For he hath not despised nor abhorred the affliction of the afflicted; neither hath he hid his face from him; but when he cried unto him, he heard.

Psalm 22:5, 24

For this shall every one that is godly pray unto thee in a time when thou mayest be found: surely in the floods of great waters they shall not come nigh unto him.

Psalm 32:6

This poor man cried, and the Lord heard him, and saved him out of all his troubles.

Psalm 34:6

And call upon me in the day of trouble: I will deliver thee, and thou shalt glorify me.

Psalm 50:15

Make haste, O God, to deliver me; make haste to help me, O Lord.

Psalm 70:1

Thou calledst in trouble, and I delivered thee; I answered thee in the secret place of thunder: I proved thee at the waters of Meribah. Selah.

Psalm 81:7

Who knoweth the power of thine anger? even according to thy fear, so is thy wrath.

So teach us to number our days, that we may apply our hearts unto wisdom.

And let the beauty of the Lord our God be upon us: and establish thou the work of our hands upon us; yea, the work of our hands establish thou it.

Psalm 90:11, 12, 17

He will regard the prayer of the destitute, and not despise their prayer.

Psalm 102:17

The Lord shall send the rod of thy strength out of Zion: rule thou in the midst of thine enemies.

Psalm 110:2

Many a time have they afflicted me from my youth: yet they have not prevailed against me.

Psalm 129:2

And, behold, there arose a great tempest in the sea, insomuch that the ship was covered with the waves: but he was asleep.

And his disciples came to him, and awoke him, saying, Lord, save us: we perish.

And he saith unto them, Why are ye fearful, O ye of little faith? Then he arose, and rebuked the winds and the sea; and there was a great calm.

Matthew 8:24-26

And Samson called unto the Lord, and said, O Lord God, remember me, I pray thee, and strengthen me, I pray thee, only this once, O God, that I may be once avenged of the Philistines for my two eyes.

And Samson took hold of the two middle pillars upon which the house stood, and on which it was borne up, of the one with his right hand, and of the other with his left.

And Samson said, Let me die with the Philistines. And he bowed himself with all his might; and the house fell upon the lords, and upon all the people that were therein. So the dead which he slew at his death were more than they which he slew in his life.

Then his brethren and all the house of his father came down and took him, and brought him up, and buried him between Zorah and Eshtaol in the burying place of Manoah his father. And he judged Israel twenty years.

Judges 16:28-31

What time I am afraid, I will trust in thee.

In God I will praise his word, in God I have put my trust; I will not fear what flesh can do unto me.

In God have I put my trust: I will not be afraid what man can do unto me.

Psalm 56:3, 4, 11

Be not afraid of sudden fear, neither of the desolation of the wicked, when it cometh.

For the Lord shall be thy confidence, and shall keep thy foot from being taken.

Proverbs 3:25, 26

For God hath not given us the spirit of fear; but of power, and of love, and of a sound mind.

II Timothy 1:7

There is no fear in love; but perfect love casteth out fear: because fear hath torment. He that feareth is not made perfect in love.

I John 4:18

Thou shalt hide them in the secret of thy presence from the pride of man: thou shalt keep them secretly in a pavilion from the strife of tongues.

Psalm 31:20

He that dwelleth in the secret place of the most High shall abide under the shadow of the Almighty.

I will say of the Lord, He is my refuge and my fortress: my God; in him will I trust.

Surely he shall deliver thee from the snare of the fowler, and from the noisome pestilence.

He shall cover thee with his feathers, and under his wings shalt thou trust: his truth shall be thy shield and buckler.

Thou shalt not be afraid for the terror by night; nor for the arrow that flieth by day;

Nor for the pestilence that walketh in darkness; nor for the destruction that wasteth at noonday.

A thousand shall fall at thy side, and ten thousand at thy right hand; but it shall not come nigh thee.

Only with thine eyes shalt thou behold and see the reward of the wicked.

Because thou hast made the Lord, which is my refuge, even the most High, thy habitation;

There shall no evil befall thee, neither shall any plague come nigh thy dwelling.

For he shall give his angels charge over thee, to keep thee in all thy ways.

They shall bear thee up in their hands, lest thou dash thy foot against a stone.

Thou shalt tread upon the lion and adder: the young lion and the dragon shalt thou trample under feet.

Because he hath set his love upon me, therefore will I deliver him: I will set him on high, because he hath known my name.

He shall call upon me, and I will answer him: I will be with him in trouble; I will deliver him, and honour him.

With long life will I satisfy him, and shew him my salvation.

Psalm 91

Thou wilt keep him in perfect peace, whose mind is stayed on thee: because he trusteth in thee.

Trust ye in the Lord for ever: for in the Lord JEHOVAH is everlasting strength:

For he bringeth down them that dwell on high; the lofty city, he layeth it low; he layeth it low, even to the ground; he bringeth it even to the dust.

The foot shall tread it down, even the feet of the poor, and the steps of the needy.

The way of the just is uprightness: thou, most upright, dost weigh the path of the just.

Yea, in the way of thy judgments, O Lord, have we waited for thee; the desire of our soul is to thy name, and to the remembrance of thee.

With my soul have I desired thee in the night; yea, with my spirit within me will I seek thee early: for when thy judgments are in the earth, the inhabitants of the world will learn righteousness.

Let favour be shewed to the wicked, yet will he not learn righteousness: in the land of uprightness will he deal unjustly, and will not behold the majesty of the Lord.

Lord, when thy hand is lifted up, they will not see: but they shall see, and be ashamed for their envy at the people; yea, the fire of thine enemies shall devour them.

Lord, thou wilt ordain peace for us: for thou also hast wrought all our works in us.

O Lord our God, other lords beside thee have had dominion over us: but by thee only will we make mention of thy name.

They are dead, they shall not live; they are deceased, they shall not rise: therefore hast thou visited and destroyed them, and made all their memory to perish.

Thou hast increased the nation, O Lord, thou hast increased the nation: thou art glorified: thou hast removed it far unto all the ends of the earth.

Lord, in trouble have they visited thee, they poured out a prayer when thy chastening was upon them.

Like as a woman with child, that draweth near the time of her delivery, is in pain, and crieth out in her pangs; so have we been in thy sight, O Lord.

We have been with child, we have been in pain, we have as it were brought forth wind; we have not wrought any deliverance in the earth; neither have the inhabitants of the world fallen.

Thy dead men shall live, together with my dead body shall they arise. Awake and sing, ye that dwell in dust: for thy dew is as the dew of herbs, and the earth shall cast out the dead.

Come, my people, enter thou into thy chambers, and shut thy doors about thee: hide thyself as it were for a little moment, until the indignation be overpast.

For, behold, the Lord cometh out of his place to punish the inhabitants of the earth for their iniquity: the earth also shall disclose her blood, and shall no more cover her slain.

Isaiah 26:3-21

No weapon that is formed against thee shall prosper; and every tongue that shall rise against thee in judgment thou shalt condemn. This is the heritage of the servants of the Lord, and their righteousness is of me, saith the Lord.

Isaiah 54:17

Peace I leave with you, my peace I give unto you: not as the world giveth, give I unto you. Let not your heart be troubled, neither let it be afraid.

John 14:27

Now the God of hope fill you with all joy and peace in believing, that ye may abound in hope, through the power of the Holy Ghost.

Romans 15:13

Finally, brethren, farewell. Be perfect, be of good comfort, be of one mind, live in peace; and the God of love and peace shall be with you.

II Corinthians 13:11

Be careful for nothing; but in every thing by prayer and supplication with thanksgiving let your requests be made known unto God.

And the peace of God, which passeth all understanding, shall keep your hearts and minds through Christ Jesus.

Philippians 4:6-7

Now the Lord of peace himself give you peace always by all means. The Lord be with you all.

II Thessalonians 3:16

Now the God of peace, that brought again from the dead our Lord Jesus, that great shepherd of the sheep, through the blood of the everlasting covenant,

Make you perfect in every good work to do his will, working in you that which is well-pleasing in his sight, through Jesus Christ; to whom be glory for ever and ever. Amen.

Hebrews 13:20-21

And when we cried unto the Lord God of our fathers, the Lord heard our voice, and looked on our affliction, and our labour, and our oppression:

And the Lord brought us forth out of Egypt with a mighty hand, and with an outstretched arm, and with great terribleness, and with signs, and with wonders:

And he hath brought us into this place, and hath given us this land, even a land that floweth with milk and honey.

Deuteronomy 26:7-9

The Lord is my light and my salvation; whom shall I fear? the Lord is the strength of my life; of whom shall I be afraid?

When the wicked, even mine enemies and my foes, came upon me to eat up my flesh, they stumbled and fell.

Though an host should encamp against me, my heart shall not fear: though war should rise against me, in this will I be confident.

Psalm 27:1-3

Prayer for Physical Healing

Then Jonah prayed unto the Lord his God out of the fish's belly,

And said, I cried by reason of mine affliction unto the Lord, and he heard me; out of the belly of hell cried I, and thou heardest my voice.

For thou hadst cast me into the deep, in the midst of the seas; and the floods compassed me about: all thy billows and thy waves passed over me.

Then I said, I am cast out of thy sight; yet I will look again toward thy holy temple.

The waters compassed me about, even to the soul: the depth closed me round about, the weeds were wrapped about my head.

I went down to the bottoms of the mountains; the earth with her bars was about me for ever: yet hast thou brought up my life from corruption, O Lord my God.

When my soul fainted within me I remembered the Lord: and my prayer came in unto thee, into thine holy temple.

They that observe lying vanities forsake their own mercy.

But I will sacrifice unto thee with the voice of thanksgiving; I will pray that that I have vowed. Salvation is of the Lord.

Jonah 2:1-9

And Abraham said unto God, O that Ishmael might live before thee.

And God said, Sarah thy wife shall bear thee a son indeed; and thou shalt call his name Isaac: and I will establish my covenant with him for an everlasting covenant, and with his seed after him.

Genesis 17:18, 19

Now therefore stand and see this great thing, which the Lord will do before your eyes.

I Samuel 12:16

And the king answered and said unto the man of God, Entreat now the face of the Lord thy God, and pray for me, that my hand may be restored me again. And the man of God besought the Lord, and the king's hand was restored him again, and became as it was before.

I Kings 13:6

And he cried unto the Lord, and said, O Lord my God, hast thou also brought evil upon the widow with whom I sojourn, by slaying her son?

And he stretched himself upon the child three times, and cried unto the Lord, and said, O Lord my God, I pray thee, let this child's soul come into him again.

And the Lord heard the voice of Elijah; and the soul of the child came into him again, and he revived.

And Elijah took the child, and brought him down out of the chamber into the house, and delivered him unto his mother: and Elijah said, See, thy son liveth.

And the woman said to Elijah, Now by this I know that thou art a man of God, and that the word of the Lord in thy mouth is truth.

I Kings 17:20-24

In those days was Hezekiah sick unto death. And the prophet Isaiah the son of Amoz came to him, and said unto him, Thus saith the Lord, Set thine house in order; for thou shalt die, and not live.

Then he turned his face to the wall, and prayed unto the Lord, saying,

I beseech thee, O Lord, remember now how I have walked before thee in truth and with a perfect heart, and have done that which is good in thy sight. And Hezekiah wept sore.

II Kings 20:1-3

O Lord my God, I cried unto thee, and thou hast healed me.

Psalm 30:2

He sent his word, and healed them, and delivered them from their destructions.

Psalm 107:20

Be not wise in thine own eyes: fear the Lord, and depart from evil.

It shall be health to thy navel, and marrow to thy bones.

Proverbs 3:7, 8

And as he entered into a certain village, there met him ten men that were lepers, which stood afar off:

And they lifted up their voices, and said, Jesus, Master, have mercy on us.

And when he saw them, he said unto them, Go shew yourselves unto the priests. And it came to pass, that, as they went, they were cleansed.

Luke 17:12-14

And when he had called unto him his twelve disciples, he gave them power against unclean spirits, to cast them out, and to heal all manner of sickness and all manner of disease.

Matthew 10:1

And to have power to heal sickness, and to cast out devils:

Mark 3:15

Then they took away the stone from the place where the dead was laid. And Jesus lifted up his eyes, and said, Father, I thank thee that thou hast heard me.

John 11:41

And he took him by the right hand, and lifted him up: and immediately his feet and ankle bones received strength.

Acts 3:7

There came also a multitude out of the cities round about unto Jerusalem, bringing sick folks, and them which were vexed with unclean spirits: and they were healed every one.

Acts 5:16

And there sat a certain man at Lystra, impotent in his feet, being a cripple from his mother's womb, who never had walked:

The same heard Paul speak: who stedfastly beholding him, and perceiving that he had faith to be healed,

Said with a loud voice, Stand upright on thy feet. And he leaped and walked.

Acts 14:8-10

But Peter put them all forth, and kneeled down, and prayed; and turning him to the body said, Tabitha, arise. And she opened her eyes: and when she saw Peter, she sat up.

And he gave her his hand, and lifted her up, and when he had called the saints and widows, presented her alive.

And it was known throughout all Joppa; and many believed in the Lord.

Acts 9:40-42

And it came to pass, as we went to prayer, a certain damsel possessed with a spirit of divination met us, which brought her masters much gain by soothsaying:

The same followed Paul and us, and cried, saying, These men are the servants of the most high God which shew unto us the way of salvation.

And this did she many days. But Paul, being grieved, turned and said to the spirit, I command thee in the name of Jesus Christ to come out of her. And he come out the same hour.

Acts 16:16-18

So that from his body were brought unto the sick handkerchiefs or aprons, and the diseases departed from them, and the evil spirits went out of them.

And God wrought special miracles by the hands of Paul:

Acts 19:11-12

And it came to pass, that the father of Publius lay sick of a fever and of a bloody flux: to whom Paul entered in, and prayed, and laid his hands on him, and healed him.

Acts 28:8

Is any sick among you? let him call the elders of the church; and let them pray over him, anointing him with oil in the name of the Lord:

James 5:14

Then said he unto me, Prophesy unto the wind, prophesy, son of man, and say to the wind, Thus saith the Lord God; Come from the four winds, O breath, and breathe upon these slain, that they may live.

So I prophesied as he commanded me, and the breath came into them, and they lived, and stood up upon their feet, an exceeding great army.

Ezekiel 37:9, 10

God's Gift of Prosperity

And God Almighty bless thee, and make thee fruitful, and multiply thee, that thou mayest be a multitude of people;

And give thee the blessing of Abraham, to thee, and to thy seed with thee; that thou mayest inherit the land wherein thou art a stranger, which God gave unto Abraham.

And Isaac sent away Jacob: and he went to Padanaram unto Laban, son of Bethuel the Syrian, the brother of Rebekah, Jacob's and Esau's mother.

When Esau saw that Isaac had blessed Jacob, and sent him away to Padanaram, to take him a wife from thence; and that as he blessed him he gave him a charge, saying, Thou shalt not take a wife of the daughters of Canaan;

And that Jacob obeyed his father and his mother, and was gone to Padanaram;

And Esau seeing that the daughters of Canaan pleased not Isaac his father;

Then went Esau unto Ishmael, and took unto the wives which he had Mahalath the daughter of Ishmael Abraham's son, the sister of Nebajoth, to be his wife.

And Jacob went out from Beersheba, and went toward Haran.

And he lighted upon a certain place, and tarried there all night, because the sun was set; and he took of the stones of that place, and put them for his pillows, and lay down in that place to sleep.

And he dreamed, and behold a ladder set up on the earth, and the top of it reached to heaven: and behold the angels of God ascending and descending on it.

And, behold, the Lord stood above it, and said, I am the Lord God of Abraham thy father, and the God of Isaac: the land whereon thou liest, to thee will I give it, and to thy seed;

Genesis 28:3-13

I am the God of Bethel, where thou anointedst the pillar, and where thou vowedst a vow unto me: now arise, get thee out from this land, and return unto the land of thy kindred.

And Rachel and Leah answered and said unto him, Is there yet any portion of inheritance for us in our father's house?

Are we not counted of him strangers? for he hath sold us, and hath quite devoured also our money.

For all the riches which God hath taken from our father, that is ours, and our children's: now then, whatsoever God hath said unto thee, do.

Genesis 31:13-16

And the LORD was with Joseph, and he was a prosperous man; and he was in the house of his master the Egyptian.

And his master saw that the LORD was with him, and that the LORD made all that he did to prosper in his hand.

But the LORD was with Joseph, and shewed him mercy, and gave him favour in the sight of the keeper of the prison.

And the keeper of the prison committed to Joseph's hand all the prisoners that were in the prison; and whatsoever they did there, he was the doer of it.

The keeper of the prison looked not to any thing that was under his hand; because the LORD was with him, and that which he did, the LORD made it to prosper.

Genesis 39:2-3, 21-23

Blessed shall be thy basket and thy store.

Blessed shalt thou be when thou comest in, and blessd shalt thou be when thou goest out.

The Lord shall cause thine enemies that rise up against thee to be smitten before thy face: they shall come out against thee one way, and flee before thee seven ways.

The Lord shall command the blessing upon thee in thy storehouses, and in all that thou settest thine hand unto; and he shall bless thee in the land which the Lord thy God giveth thee.

The Lord shall establish thee an holy people unto himself, as he hath sworn unto thee, if thou shalt keep the commandments of the Lord thy God, and walk in his ways.

And all people of the earth shall see that thou art called by the name of the Lord; and they shall be afraid of thee.

And the Lord shall make thee plenteous in goods, in the fruit of thy body, and in the fruit of thy cattle, and in the fruit of thy ground, in the land which the Lord sware unto thy fathers to give thee.

The Lord shall open unto thee his good treasure, the heaven to give the rain unto thy land in his season, and to bless all the work of thine hand: and thou shalt lend unto many nations, and thou shalt not borrow.

And the Lord shall make thee the head and not the tail; and thou shalt be above only, and thou shalt not be beneath; if that thou hearken unto the commandments of the Lord thy God, which I command thee this day, to observe and to do them:

And thou shalt not go aside from any of the words which I command thee this day, to the right hand, or to the left, to go after other gods to serve them.

Deuteronomy 28:5-14

Only be thou strong and very courageous, that thou mayest observe to do according to all the law, which Moses my servant commanded thee:

This book of the law shall not depart out of thy mouth; but thou shalt meditate therein day and night, that thou mayest observe to do according to all that is written therein: for then thou shalt make thy way prosperous, and then thou shalt have good success.

Have not I commanded thee? Be strong and of a good courage; be not afraid, neither be thou dismayed: for the Lord thy God is with thee whithersoever thou goest.

Joshua 1:7-9

And Solomon told her all her questions: there was not any thing hid from the king, which he told her not.

And when the queen of Sheba had seen all Solomon's wisdom, and the house that he had built,

And the meat of his table, and the sitting of his servants, and the attendance of his ministers, and their apparel, and his cupbearers, and his ascent by which he went up unto the house of the Lord; there was no more spirit in her.

And she said to the king, It was a true report that I heard in mine own land of thy acts and of thy wisdom.

Howbeit I believed not the words, until I came, and mine eyes had seen it: and, behold, the half was not told me: thy wisdom and prosperity exceedeth the fame which I heard.

I Kings 10:3-7

And when David had made an end of offering the burnt offerings and the peace offerings, he blessed the people in the name of the Lord.

I Chronicles 16:2

And Hezekiah appointed the courses of the priests and the Levites after their courses, every man according to his service, the priests and Levites for burnt offering and for peace offerings, to minister, and to give thanks, and to praise in the gates of the tents of the Lord.

II Chronicles 31:2

This same Hezekiah also stopped the upper watercourse of Gihon, and brought it straight down to the west side of the city of David. And Hezekiah prospered in all his works.

II Chronicles 32:30

And it was so, that after the Lord had spoken these words unto Job, the Lord said to Eliphaz the Temanite, My wrath is kindled against thee, and against thy two friends: for ye have not spoken of me the thing that is right, as my servant Job hath.

Therefore take unto you now seven bullocks and seven rams, and go to my servant Job, and offer up for yourselves a burnt offering; and my servant Job shall pray for you: for him will I accept: lest I deal with you after your folly, in that ye have not spoken of me the thing which is right, like my servant Job.

So Eliphaz the Temanite and Bildad the Shuhite and Zophar the Naamathite went, and did according as the Lord commanded them: the Lord also accepted Job.

And the Lord turned the captivity of Job, when he prayed for his friends: also the Lord gave Job twice as much as he had before.

Job 42:7-10

And he shall be like a tree planted by the rivers of water, that bringeth forth his fruit in his season; his leaf also shall not wither; and whatsoever he doeth shall prosper.

Psalm 1:3

And in my prosperity I said, I shall never be moved.

Lord, by thy favour thou hast made my mountain to stand strong: thou didst hide thy face, and I was troubled.

I cried to thee, O Lord; and unto the Lord I made supplication.

Psalm 30:6-8

For the Lord God is a sun and shield: the Lord will give grace and glory: no good thing will he withhold from them that walk uprightly.

Psalm 84:11

He brought them forth also with silver and gold: and there was not one feeble person among their tribes.

Psalm 105:37

He raiseth up the poor out of the dust, and lifteth the needy out of the dunghill;

That he may set him with princes, even with the princes of his people.

Psalm 113:7-8

Be not wise in thine own eyes: fear the LORD, and depart from evil.

It shall be health to thy navel, and marrow to thy bones.

Honour the LORD with thy substance, and with the firstfruits of all thine increase:

So shall thy barns be filled with plenty, and thy presses shall burst out with new wine.

Proverbs 3:7-10

He that giveth unto the poor shall not lack: but he that hideth his eyes shall have many a curse.

Proverbs 28:27

For what hath the wise more than the fool? what hath the poor, that knoweth to walk before the living?

Ecclesiastes 6:8

Cast thy bread upon the waters: for thou shalt find it after many days.

Ecclesiastes 11:1

And I will give thee treasures of darkness, and hidden riches of secret places, that thou mayest know that I, the Lord, which call thee by thy name, am the God of Israel.

Isaiah 45:3

Then shalt thou delight thyself in the Lord; and I will cause thee to ride upon the high places of the earth, and feed thee with the heritage of Jacob thy father: for the mouth of the Lord hath spoken it.

Isaiah 58:14

And I will gather the remnant of my flock out of all countries whither I have driven them, and will bring them again to their folds; and they shall be fruitful and increase.

And I will set up shepherds over them which shall feed them: and they shall fear no more, nor be dismayed, neither shall they be lacking, saith the Lord.

Behold, the days come, saith the Lord, that I will raise unto David a righteous Branch, and a King shall reign and prosper, and shall execute judgment and justice in the earth.

In his days Judah shall be saved, and Israel shall dwell safely; and this is his name whereby he shall be called, THE LORD OUR RIGHTEOUSNESS.

Therefore, behold, the days come, saith the Lord, that they shall no more say, The Lord liveth, which brought up the children of Israel out of the land of Egypt;

But, The Lord liveth, which brought up and which led the seed of the house of Israel out of the north country, and from all countries whither I had driven them; and they shall dwell in their own land.

Jeremiah 23:3-8

So this Daniel prospered in the reign of Darius, and in the reign of Cyrus the Persian.

Daniel 6:28

And Jesus answered and said, Verily I say unto you, There is no man that hath left house, or brethren, or sisters, or father, or mother, or wife, or children, or lands, for my sake, and the gospel's,

But he shall receive an hundredfold now in this time, houses, and brethren, and sisters, and mothers, and children, and lands, with persecutions; and in the world to come eternal life.

But many that are first shall be last; and the last first.

Mark 10:29-31

But seek ye first the kingdom of God, and his righteousness; and all these things shall be added unto you.

Matthew 6:33

For ye know the grace of our Lord Jesus Christ, that, though he was rich, yet for your sakes he became poor, that ye through his poverty might be rich.

II Corinthians 8:9

But my God shall supply all your need according to his riches in glory by Christ Jesus.

Philippians 4:19

Then he took the five loaves and the two fishes, and looking up to heaven, he blessed them, and brake, and gave to the disciples to set before the multitude.

Luke 9:16

And Jesus took the loaves; and when he had given thanks, he distributed to the disciples, and the disciples to them that were set down; and likewise of the fishes as much as they would.

John 6:11

Charge them that are rich in this world, that they be not highminded, nor trust in uncertain riches, but in the living God, who giveth us richly all things to enjoy;

I Timothy 6:17

Beloved, I wish above all things that thou mayest prosper and be in health, even as thy soul prospereth.

III John 2

Ask ye of the Lord rain in the time of the latter rain; so the Lord shall make bright clouds, and give them showers of rain, to every one grass in the field.

Zechariah 10:1

And Elijah said unto Ahab, Get thee up, eat and drink; for there is a sound of abundance of rain.

So Ahab went up to eat and to drink. And Elijah went up to the top of Carmel; and he cast himself down upon the earth, and put his face between his knees.

And said to his servant, Go up now, look toward the sea. And he went up, and looked, and said, There is nothing. And he said, Go again seven times.

And it came to pass at the seventh time, that he said, Behold, there ariseth a little cloud out of the sea, like a man's hand. And he said, Go up, say unto Ahab, Prepare thy chariot, and get thee down, that the rain stop thee not.

And it came to pass in the mean while, that the heaven was black with clouds and wind, and there was a great rain. And Ahab rode, and went to Jezreel.

And the hand of the Lord was on Elijah; and he girded up his loins, and ran before Ahab to the entrance of Jezreel.

I Kings 18:41-46

Then I will give you rain in due season, and the land shall yield her increase, and the trees of the field shall yield their fruit.

And your threshing shall reach unto the vintage, and the vintage shall reach unto the sowing time: and ye shall eat your bread to the full, and dwell in your land safely.

Leviticus 26:4, 5

Promise of Revival

But when he saw the multitudes, he was moved with compassion on them, because they fainted, and were scattered abroad, as sheep having no shepherd.

Then saith he unto his disciples, The harvest is plenteous, but the labourers are few;

Pray ye therefore the Lord of the harvest, that he will send forth labourers into his harvest.

Matthew 9:36-38

Say not ye, There are yet four months, and then cometh harvest? behold, I say unto you, Lift up your eyes, and look on the fields; for they are white already to harvest.

And he that reapeth receiveth wages, and gathereth fruit unto life eternal: that both he that soweth and he that reapeth may rejoice together.

And herein is that saying true, One soweth, and another reapeth.

I sent you to reap that whereon ye bestowed no labour: other men laboured, and ye are entered into their labours.

And many of the Samaritans of that city believed on him for the saying of the woman, which testified, He told me all that ever I did.

So when the Samaritans were come unto him, they besought him that he would tarry with them: and he abode there two days.

And many more believed because of his own word;

And said unto the woman, Now we believe, not because of thy saying: for we have heard him ourselves, and know that this is indeed the Christ, the Saviour of the world.

John 4:35-42

Restore unto me the joy of thy salvation; and uphold me with thy free spirit.

Then will I teach transgressors thy ways; and sinners shall be converted unto thee.

Psalm 51:12, 13

Wilt thou not revive us again: that thy people may rejoice in thee?

Psalm 85:6

It is time for thee, Lord, to work: for they have made void thy law.

Psalm 119:126

Call unto me, and I will answer thee, and shew thee great and mighty things, which thou knowest not.

Jeremiah 33:3

If I shut up heaven that there be no rain, or if I command the locusts to devour the land, or if I send pestilence among my people;

If my people, which are called by my name, shall humble themselves, and pray, and seek my face, and turn from their wicked ways; then will I hear from heaven, and will forgive their sin, and will heal their land.

II Chronicles 7:13, 14

Be glad then, ye children of Zion, and rejoice in the Lord your God: for he hath given you the former rain moderately, and he will cause to come down for you the rain, the former rain, and the latter rain in the first month.

And the floors shall be full of wheat, and the vats shall overflow with wine and oil.

And I will restore to you the years that the locust hath eaten, the cankerworm, and the caterpillar, and the palmerworm, my great army which I sent among you.

And ye shall eat in plenty, and be satisfied, and praise the name of the Lord your God, that hath dealt wondrously with you: and my people shall never be ashamed.

And ye shall know that I am in the midst of Israel, and that I am the Lord your God, and none else: and my people shall never be ashamed.

And it shall come to pass afterward, that I will pour out my spirit upon all flesh; and your sons and your daughters shall prophesy, your old men shall dream dreams, your young men shall see visions:

And also upon the servants and upon the handmaids in those days will I pour out my spirit.

Joel 2:23-29

The spirit of the Lord God is upon me; because the Lord hath anointed me to preach good tidings unto the meek; he hath sent me to bind up the brokenhearted, to proclaim liberty to the captives, and the opening of the prison to them that are bound;

But ye shall be named the Priests of the Lord: men shall call you the Ministers of our God: ye shall eat the riches of the Gentiles, and in their glory shall ye boast yourselves.

Isaiah 61:1, 6

A PRAYER of Habbakkuk the prophet upon Shigionoth.

O Lord, I have heard thy speech, and was afraid: O LORD, revive thy work in the midst of the years, in the midst of the years make known; in wrath remember mercy.

God came from Teman, and the Holy One from mount Paran. Selah.

His glory covered the heavens, and the earth was full of his praise.

Habakkuk 3:1-3

And he is the propitiation for our sins: and not for ours only, but also for the sins of the whole world.

I John 2:2

Prayer for Guidance

And call upon me in the day of trouble: I will deliver thee, and thou shalt glorify me.

Psalm 50:15

When I cry unto thee, then shall mine enemies turn back: this I know; for God is for me.

Psalm 56:9

Trust in him at all times; ye people, pour out your heart before him: God is a refuge for us. Selah.

Psalm 62:8

Lead me, O Lord, in thy righteousness because of mine enemies: make thy way straight before my face.

Psalm 5:8

He maketh me to lie down in green pastures: he leadeth me beside the still waters.

Psalm 23:2

Lead me in thy truth, and teach me: for thou art the God of my salvation; on thee do I wait all the day.

The meek will he guide in judgment: and the meek will he teach his way.

Psalm 25:5, 9

Teach me thy way, O Lord, and lead me in a plain path, because of mine enemies.

Psalm 27:11

For this God is our God for ever and ever: he will be our guide even unto death.

Psalm 48:14

Therefore David inquired of the Lord, saying, Shall I go and smite these Philistines? And the Lord said unto David, Go, and smite the Philistines, and save Keilah.

Then said David, O Lord God of Israel, thy servant hath certainly heard that Saul seeketh to come to Keilah, to destroy the city for my sake.

Will the men of Keilah deliver me up into his hand? will Saul come down, as thy servant hath heard? O Lord God of Israel, I beseech thee, tell thy servant. And the Lord said, He will come down.

Then said David, Will the men of Keilah deliver me and my men into the hand of Saul? And the Lord said, They will deliver thee up.

And David abode in the wilderness in strong holds, and remained in a mountain in the wilderness of Ziph. And Saul sought him everyday, but God delivered him not into his hand.

I Samuel 23:2, 10-12, 14

Then shalt thou call, and the Lord shall answer; thou shalt cry, and he shall say, Here I am. If thou take away from the midst of thee thy yoke, the putting forth of the finger, and speaking vanity;

And if thou draw out thy soul to the hungry and satisfy the afflicted Saul; then shall thy light rise in obscurity, and thy darkness be as the noon day.

And the LORD shall guide thee continually, and satisfy thy soul in drought, and make fat thy bones: and thou shalt be like a watered garden, and like a spring of water, whose waters fail not.

Isaiah 58:9-11

When they had heard the king, they departed; and, lo, the star, which they saw in the east, went before them, till it came and stood over where the young child was.

Matthew 2:9

Thou shalt guide me with thy counsel, and afterward receive me to glory.

Psalm 73:24

In the daytime also he led them with a cloud, and all the night with a light of fire.

Psalm 78:14

Teach me, O Lord, the way of thy statutes; and I shall keep it unto the end.

Psalm 119:33

Teach me to do thy will; for thou art God: thy spirit is good; lead me into the land of uprightness.

Psalm 143:10

And I will bring the blind by a way that they knew not; I will lead them in paths that they have not known: I will make darkness light before them, and crooked things straight. These things will I do unto them, and not forsake them.

Isaiah 42:16

Be strong and of a good courage, fear not, nor be afraid of them: for the Lord thy God, he it is that doth go with thee; he will not fail thee, nor forsake thee.

Deuteronomy 31:6

(And the children of Israel went up and wept before the Lord until even, and asked counsel of the Lord, saying, Shall I go up again to battle against the children of Benjamin my brother? And the Lord said, Go up against him.)

And the children of Israel came near against the children of Benjamin the second day.

And Benjamin went forth against them out of Gibeah the second day, and destroyed down to the ground of the children of Israel again eighteen thousand men; all these drew the sword.

Then all the children of Israel, and all the people, went up, and came unto the house of God, and went and sat there before the Lord, and fasted that day until even, and offered burnt offerings and peace offerings before the Lord.

And the children of Israel inquired of the Lord, (for the ark of the covenant of God was there in those days,

And Phinehas, the son of Eleazar, the son of Aaron, stood before it in those days,) saying, Shall I yet again go out to battle against the children of Benjamin my brother, or shall I cease? And the Lord said, Go up; for tomorrow I will deliver them into thine hand.

Judges 20:23-28

And the Lord called Samuel again the third time. And he arose and went to Eli, and said, Here am I; for thou didst call me. And Eli perceived that the Lord had called the child.

Therefore Eli said unto Samuel, Go, lie down: and it shall be, if he call thee, that thou shalt say, Speak, Lord; for thy servant heareth. So Samuel went and lay down in his place.

And the Lord came, and stood, and called as at other times, Samuel, Samuel. Then Samuel answered, Speak; for thy servant heareth.

I Samuel 3:8-10

Preparation For Prayer

Meditation in God's Word

This book of the law shall not depart out of thy mouth; but thou shalt meditate therein day and night, that thou mayest observe to do according to all that is written therein: for then thou shalt make thy way prosperous, and then thou shalt have good success.

Joshua 1:8

Blessed is the man that walketh not in the counsel of the ungodly, nor standeth in the way of sinners, nor sitteth in the seat of the scornful.

But his delight is in the law of the Lord; and in his law doth he meditate day and night.

And he shall be like a tree planted by the rivers of water, that bringeth forth his fruit in his season; his leaf also shall not wither; and whatsoever he doeth shall prosper.

Psalm 1:1-3

Give ear to my words, O Lord, consider my meditation.

Hearken unto the voice of my cry, my King, and my God: for unto thee will I pray.

My voice shalt thou hear in the morning, O Lord; in the morning will I direct my prayer unto thee, and will look up.

Psalm 5:1-3

Let the words of my mouth, and the meditation of my heart, be acceptable in thy sight, O Lord, my strength, and my redeemer.

Psalm 19:14

My mouth shall speak of wisdom; and the meditation of my heart shall be of understanding.

Psalm 49:3

When I remember thee upon my bed, and meditate on thee in the night watches.

Because thou hast been my help, therefore in the shadow of thy wings will I rejoice.

My soul followeth hard after thee: thy right hand upholdeth me.

Psalm 63:6-8

I will meditate also of all thy work, and talk of thy doings.

Thy way, O God, is in the sanctuary: who is so great a God as our God?

Thou art the God that doest wonders: thou hast declared thy strength among the people.

Thou hast with thine arm redeemed thy people, the sons of Jacob and Joseph. Selah.

Psalm 77:12-15

I will sing unto the Lord as long as I live: I will sing praise to my God while I have my being.

My meditation of him shall be sweet: I will be glad in the Lord.

Psalm 104:33-34

I will meditate in thy precepts, and have respect unto thy ways.

I will delight myself in thy statutes: I will not forget thy word.

Princes also did sit and speak against me: but thy servant did meditate in thy statutes.

Thy testimonies also are my delight and my counsellors.

My soul cleaveth unto the dust: quicken thou me according to thy word.

Psalm 119:15-16, 23-25

My hands also will I lift up unto thy commandments, which I have loved; and I will meditate in thy statutes.

Let thy tender mercies come unto me, that I may live: for thy law is my delight.

Let the proud be ashamed; for they dealt perversely with me without a cause: but I will meditate in thy precepts.

Psalm 119:48. 77-78

O how love I thy law! it is my meditation all the day.

Thou through thy commandments hast made me wiser than mine enemies: for they are ever with me.

I have more understanding than all my teachers: for thy testimonies are my meditation.

Psalm 119:97-99

I cried with my whole heart; hear me, O Lord; I will keep thy statutes.

I cried unto thee; save me, and I shall keep thy testimonies.

I prevented the dawning of the morning, and cried: I hoped in thy word.

Mine eyes prevent the night watches, that I might meditate in thy word.

Hear my voice according unto thy lovingkindness: O Lord, quicken me according to thy judgment.

Psalm 119:145-149

I remember the days of old; I meditate on all thy works; I muse on the work of thy hand.

Psalm 143:5

Finally, brethren, whatsoever things are true, whatsoever things are honest, whatsoever things are just, whatsoever things are pure, whatsoever things are lovely, whatsoever things are of good report; if there be any virtue, and if there be any praise, think on these things.

Those things which ye have both learned, and received, and heard, and seen in me, do: and the God of peace shall be with you.

Philippians 4:8-9

Till I come, give attendance to reading, to exhortation, to doctrine.

Neglect not the gift that is in thee, which was given thee by prophecy, with the laying on of the hands of the presbytery.

Meditate upon these things; give thyself wholly to them; that thy profiting may appear to all.

Take heed unto thyself, and unto the doctrine; continue in them: for in doing this thou shalt both save thyself, and them that hear thee.

I Timothy 4:13-16

Ministering to God

But Samuel ministered before the Lord, being a child, girded with a linen ephod.

I Samuel 2:18

And the child Samuel ministered unto the Lord before Eli. And the word of the Lord was precious in those days; there was no open vision.

I Samuel 3:1

And they ministered before the dwelling place of the tabernacle of the congregation with singing, until Solomon had built the house of the Lord in Jerusalem: and then they waited on their office according to their order.

I Chronicles 6:32

Because they ministered unto them before their idols, and caused the house of Israel to fall into iniquity; therefore have I lifted up mine hand against them, saith the Lord GOD, and they shall bear their iniquity.

And they shall not come near unto me, to do the office of a priest unto me, nor to come near to any of my holy things, in the most holy place: but they shall bear their shame, and their abominations which they have committed.

But I will make them keepers of the charge of the house, for all the service thereof, and for all that shall be done therein.

But the priests the Levites, the sons of Zadok, that kept the charge of my sanctuary when the children of Israel went astray from me, they shall come near to me to minister unto me, and they shall stand before me to offer unto me the fat and the blood, saith the Lord GOD:

They shall enter into my sanctuary, and they shall come near to my table, to minister unto me, and they shall keep my charge.

Ezekiel 44:12-16

And the King shall answer and say unto them, Verily I say unto you, Inasmuch as ye have done it unto one of the least of these my brethren, ye have done it unto me.

Matthew 25:40

As they ministered to the Lord, and fasted, the Holy Ghost said, Separate me Barnabas and Saul for the work whereunto I have called them.

Acts 13:2

For God is not unrighteous to forget your work and labour of love, which ye have shewed toward his name, in that ye have ministered to the saints, and do minister.

Hebrews 6:10

Fasting

Then I proclaimed a fast there, at the river of Ahava, that we might afflict ourselves before our God, to seek of him a right way for us, and for our little ones, and for all our substance.

For I was ashamed to require of the king a band of soldiers and horsemen to help us against the enemy in the way: because we had spoken unto the king, saying, The hand of our God is upon all them for good that seek him; but his power and his wrath is against all them that forsake him.

So we fasted and besought our God for this: and he was entreated of us.

Ezra 8:21-23

Then Ezra rose up from before the house of God, and went into the chamber of Johanan the son of Eliashib: and when he came thither, he did eat no bread, nor drink water: for he mourned because of the transgression of them that had been carried away.

Ezra 10:6

And it came to pass, when I heard these words, that I sat down and wept, and mourned certain days, and fasted, and prayed before the God of heaven,

Nehemiah 1:4

Go, gather together all the Jews that are present in Shushan, and fast ye for me, and neither eat nor drink three days, night or day: I also and my maidens will fast likewise; and so will I go in unto the king, which is not according to the law: and if I perish, I perish.

Esther 4:16

He is chastened also with pain upon his bed, and the multitude of his bones with strong pain:

So that his life abhorreth bread, and his soul dainty meat.

Job 33:19, 20

When I wept, and chastened my soul with fasting, that was to my reproach.

Psalm 69:10

My heart is smitten, and withered like grass; so that I forget to eat my bread.

Psalm 102:4

Is not this the fast that I have chosen? to loose the bands of wickedness, to undo the heavy burdens, and to let the oppressed go free, and that ye break every yoke?

Isaiah 58:6

And I set my face unto the Lord God, to seek by prayer and supplications, with fasting, and sackcloth, and ashes:

And whiles I was speaking, and praying, and confessing my sin and the sin of my people Israel, and presenting my supplication before the Lord my God for the holy mountain of my God;

Yea, whiles I was speaking in prayer, even the man Gabriel whom I had seen in the vision at the beginning, being caused to fly swiftly, touched me about the time of evening oblation.

And he informed me, and talked with me, and said, O Daniel, I am now come forth to give thee skill and understanding.

At the beginning of thy supplications the commandment came forth, and I am come to shew thee; for thou art greatly beloved: therefore understand the matter, and consider the vision.

Daniel 9:3, 20-23

I ate no pleasant bread, neither came flesh nor wine in my mouth, neither did I anoint myself at all, till three whole weeks were fulfilled.

Daniel 10:3

Blow the trumpet in Zion, sanctify a fast, call a solemn assembly:

Joel 2:15

So the people of Nineveh believed God, and proclaimed a fast, and put on sackcloth, from the greatest of them even to the least of them.

And God saw their works, that they turned from their evil way; and God repented of the evil, that he had said that he would do unto them; and he did it not.

Jonah 3:5, 10

And when he had fasted forty days and forty nights, he was afterward an hungered.

Matthew 4:2

Moreover when ye fast, be not, as the hypocrites, of a sad countenance: for they disfigure their faces, that they may appear unto men to fast. Verily I say unto you, They have their reward.

Matthew 6:16

And Jesus said unto them, Can the children of the bridechamber mourn, as long as the bridegroom is with them? but the days will come, when the bridegroom shall be taken from them, and then shall they fast.

Matthew 9:15

And when they had fasted and prayed, and laid their hands on them, they sent them away.

Acts 13:3

And when they had ordained them elders in every church, and had prayed with fasting, they commended them to the Lord, on whom they believed.

Acts 14:23

Defraud ye not one the other, except it be with consent for a time, that ye may give yourselves to fasting and prayer; and come together again, that Satan tempt you not for your incontinency.

I Corinthians 7:5

In weariness and painfulness, in watchings often, in hunger and thirst, in fastings often, in cold and nakedness.

Besides those things that are without, that which cometh upon me daily, the care of all the churches.

II Corinthians 11:27-28

And he was there with the Lord forty days and forty nights; he did neither eat bread, nor drink water. And he wrote upon the tables the words of the covenant, the ten commandments.

Exodus 34:28

When I was gone up into the mount to receive the tables of stone, even the tables of the covenant which the Lord made with you, then I abode in the mount forty days and forty nights, I neither did eat bread nor drink water.

Deuteronomy 9:9

David therefore besought God for the child;
and David fasted, and went in, and lay all night
upon the earth.

And the elders of his house arose, and went
to him, to raise him up from the earth: but he
would not, neither did he eat bread with them.

II Samuel 12:16, 17

Praise

It came even to pass, as the trumpeters and singers were as one, to make one sound to be heard in praising and thanking the Lord; and when they lifted up their voice with the trumpets and cymbals and instruments of music, and praised the Lord, saying, For he is good; for his mercy endureth for ever: that then the house was filled with a cloud, even the house of the Lord:

So that the priests could not stand to minister by reason of the cloud: for the glory of the LORD had filled the house of God.

II Chronicles 5:13-14

But let all those that put their trust in thee rejoice: let them ever shout for joy, because thou defendest them: let them also that love thy name be joyful in thee.

Psalm 5:11

I will praise thee, O Lord, with my whole heart; I will shew forth all thy marvellous works.

I will be glad and rejoice in thee: I will sing praise to thy name, O thou most High.

Psalm 9:1, 2

I will sing unto the Lord, because he hath dealt bountifully with me.

Psalm 13:6

I will call upon the Lord, who is worthy to be praised: so shall I be saved from mine enemies.

Psalm 18:3

Therefore will I give thanks unto thee, O Lord, among the heathen, and sing praises unto thy name.

Psalm 18:49

But thou art holy, O thou that inhabitest the praises of Israel.

Psalm 22:3

I will declare thy name unto my brethren: in the midst of the congregation will I praise thee.

Psalm 22:22

Give unto the Lord the glory due unto his name; worship the Lord in the beauty of holiness.

Psalm 29:2

Be glad in the Lord, and rejoice, ye righteous: and shout for joy all ye that are upright in heart.

Psalm 32:11

Rejoice in the Lord, O ye righteous: for praise is comely for the upright.

Psalm 33:1

I will bless the Lord at all times: his praise shall continually be in my mouth.

Psalm 34:1

I will give thee thanks in the great congregation: I will praise thee among much people.

Psalm 35:18

Let them shout for joy, and be glad, that favour my righteous cause: yea, let them say continually, Let the Lord be magnified, which hath pleasure in the prosperity of his servant.

Psalm 35:27

And my tongue shall speak of thy righteousness and of thy praise all day long.

Psalm 35:28

And he hath put a new song in my mouth, even praise unto our God: many shall see it, and fear, and shall trust in the Lord.

Psalm 40:3

Why art thou cast down, O my soul? and why art thou disquieted within me? hope thou in God: for I shall yet praise him, who is the health of my countenance, and my God.

Psalm 42:11

In God we boast all the day long, and praise thy name for ever. Selah.

Psalm 44:8

O clap your hands, all ye people; shout unto God with the voice of triumph.

Psalm 47:1

Sing praises to God, sing praises: sing praises unto our King, sing praises.

Psalm 47:6

Great is the Lord, and greatly to be praised in the city of our God, in the mountain of his holiness.

Psalm 48:1

Whoso offereth praise glorifieth me: and to him that ordereth his conversation aright will I shew the salvation of God.

Psalm 50:23

I will praise thee for ever, because thou hast done it: and I will wait on thy name; for it is good before thy saints.

Psalm 52:9

I will freely sacrifice unto thee: I will praise thy name, O Lord; for it is good.

Psalm 54:6

In God will I praise his word, in God I have put my trust; I will not fear what flesh can do unto me.

Psalm 56:4

In God will I praise his word: in the Lord will I praise his word.

Psalm 56:10

Thy vows are upon me, O God: I will render praises unto thee.

Psalm 56:12

My heart is fixed, O God, my heart is fixed: I will sing and give praise.

Psalm 57:7

I will praise thee, O Lord, among the people: I will sing unto thee among the nations.

Psalm 57:9

Because thy lovingkindness is better than life, my lips shall praise thee.

Psalm 63:3

Thus will I bless thee while I live: I will lift up my hands in thy name.

Psalm 63:4

Sing forth the honour of his name; make his praise glorious.

Psalm 66:2

O bless our God, ye people, and make the voice of his praise to be heard.

Psalm 66:8

Let the people praise thee, O God; let all the people praise thee.

Psalm 67:3

Blessed be the Lord, who daily loadeth us with benefits, even the God of our salvation. Selah.

Psalm 68:19

I will praise the name of God with a song, and will magnify him with thanksgiving.

Psalm 69:30

Let my mouth be filled with thy praise and with thy honour all the day.

Psalm 71:8

But I will hope continually, and will yet praise thee more and more.

Psalm 71:14

O let not the oppressed return ashamed: let the poor and needy praise thy name.

Psalm 74:21

So we thy people and sheep of thy pasture will give thee thanks for ever: we will shew forth thy praise to all generations.

Psalm 79:13

Who can utter the mighty acts of the Lord? who can shew forth all his praise?

Psalm 106:2

Then believed they his words; they sang his praise.

Psalm 106:12

Oh that men would praise the Lord for his goodness, and for his wonderful works to the children of men.

Psalm 107:8

From the rising of the sun unto the going down of the same the Lord's name is to be praised.

Psalm 113:3

My lips shall utter praise, when thou hast taught me thy statutes.

Psalm 119:171

Lift your hands in the sanctuary, and bless the Lord.

Psalm 134:2

I will praise thee with my whole heart: before the gods will I sing praise unto thee.

Psalm 138:1

I will extol thee, my God, O king; and I will bless thy name for ever and ever.

Every day will I bless thee, and I will praise thy name for ever and ever.

Great is the Lord, and greatly to be praised; and his greatness is unsearchable.

Psalm 145:1-3

My mouth shall speak the praise of the Lord: and let all flesh bless his holy name for ever and ever.

Psalm 145:21

Praise ye the Lord: for it is good to sing praises unto our God; for it is pleasant; and praise is comely.

Psalm 147:1

Sing unto the Lord with thanksgiving; sing praise upon the harp unto our God:

Psalm 147:7

Praise ye the Lord. Sing unto the Lord a new song, and his praise in the congregation of saints.

Psalm 149:1

Praise ye the Lord. Praise God in his sanctuary: praise him in the firmament of his power.
Praise him for his mighty acts: praise him according to his excellent greatness.

Psalm 150:1, 2

Let every thing that hath breath praise the Lord. Praise ye the Lord.

Psalm 150:6

O Lord, thou art my God; I will exalt thee, I will praise thy name; for thou hast done wonderful things; thy counsels of old are faithfulness and truth.

Isaiah 25:1

And one of them, when he saw that he was healed, turned back, and with a loud voice glorified God,

And fell down on his face at his feet, giving him thanks: and he was a Samaritan.

Luke 17:15, 16

And immediately he received his sight, and followed him, glorifying God: and all the people, when they saw it, gave praise unto God.

Luke 18:43

And when he was come nigh, even now at the descent of the mount of Olives, the whole multitude of the disciples began to rejoice and praise God with a loud voice for all the mighty works that they had seen;

Saying, Blessed by the King that cometh in the name of the Lord: peace in heaven, and glory in the highest.

Luke 19:37, 38

And they worshipped him, and returned to Jerusalem with great joy:

And were continually in the temple, praising and blessing God. Amen.

Luke 24:52-53

And they, continuing daily with one accord in the temple, and breaking bread from house to house, did eat their meat with gladness and singleness of heart.

Praising God, and having favour with all the people. And the Lord added to the church daily such as should be saved.

Acts 2:46-47

And he leaping up stood, and walked, and entered with them into the temple, walking, and leaping, and praising God.

Acts 3:8

And at midnight Paul and Silas prayed, and sang praises unto God: and the prisoners heard them.

Acts 16:25

But ye are a chosen generation, a royal priesthood, an holy nation, a peculiar people; that ye should shew forth the praises of him who hath called you out of darkness into his marvellous light.

I Peter 2:9

And a voice came out of the throne, saying, Praise our God, all ye his servants, and ye that fear him, both small and great.

Revelation 19:5

O Lord, open thou my lips; and my mouth shall shew forth thy praise.

Psalm 51:15

Thanksgiving

Give thanks unto the Lord, call upon his name, make known his deeds among the people.

I Chronicles 16:8

Then I brought up the princes of Judah upon the wall, and appointed two great companies of them that gave thanks, whereof one went on the right hand upon the wall toward the dung gate:

Nehemiah 12:31

Offer unto God thanksgiving; and pay thy vows unto the most High:

Psalm 50:14

Make a joyful noise unto the Lord, all ye lands.

Serve the Lord with gladness: come before his presence with singing.

Know ye that the Lord he is God: it is he that hath made us, and not we ourselves; we are his people, and the sheep of his pasture.

Enter into his gates with thanksgiving, and into his courts with praise: be thankful unto him, and bless his name.

Psalm 100:1-4

I will offer to thee the sacrifice of thanksgiving, and will call upon the name of the Lord.

Psalm 116:17

O give thanks unto the God of heaven: for his mercy endureth for ever.

Psalm 136:26

In every thing give thanks: for this is the will of God in Christ Jesus concerning you.

I Thessalonians 5:18

For every creature of God is good, and nothing to be refused, if it be received with thanksgiving.

I Timothy 4:4

By him therefore let us offer the sacrifice of praise to God continually, that is, the fruit of our lips giving thanks to his name.

Hebrews 13:15

And were continually in the temple, praising and blessing God. Amen.

Luke 24:53

Speaking to yourselves in psalms and hymns and spiritual songs, singing and making melody in your heart to the Lord.

Giving thanks always for all things unto God and the Father in the name of our Lord Jesus Christ;

Ephesians 5:19-20

Be careful for nothing; but in every thing by prayer and supplication with thanksgiving let your requests be made known unto God.

Colossians 4:2

Attitudes for Prayer

Forgiveness

Thou hast also given me the necks of mine enemies, that I might destroy them that hate me.

They looked, but there was none to save; even unto the Lord, but he answered them not.

It is God that avengeth me, and that bringeth down the people under me.

II Samuel 22:41, 42, 48

For if ye forgive men their trespasses, your heavenly Father will also forgive you.

Matthew 6:14

And when ye stand praying, forgive, if ye have aught against any: that your Father also which is in heaven may forgive you your trespasses.

But if ye do not forgive, neither will your Father which is in heaven forgive your trespasses.

Mark 11:25, 26

Then said Jesus, Father, forgive them; for they know not what they do. And they parted his raiment, and cast lots.

Luke 23:34

Forbearing one another, and forgiving one another, if any man have a quarrel against any: even as Christ forgave you, so also do ye.

Colossians 3:13

To the praise of the glory of his grace, wherein he hath made us accepted in the beloved.

In whom we have redemption through his blood, the forgiveness of sins, according to the riches of his grace;

Ephesians 1:6, 7

Thou hast forgiven the iniquity of thy people, thou hast covered all their sin. Selah.

Psalm 85:2

Therefore if any man be in Christ, he is a new creature: old things are passed away; behold, all things are become new.

II Corinthians 5:17

As far as the east is from the west, so far hath he removed our transgressions from us.

Psalm 103:12

My little children, these things write I unto you, that ye sin not. And if any man sin, we have an advocate with the Father, Jesus Christ the righteous:

I John 2:1

If we confess our sins, he is faithful and just to forgive us our sins, and to cleanse us from all unrighteousness.

I John 1:19

For I will be merciful to their unrighteousness, and their sins and their iniquities will I remember no more.

Hebrews 8:12

Obedience

If ye will fear the Lord, and serve him, and obey his voice, and not rebel against the commandment of the Lord, then shall both ye and also the king that reigneth over you continue following the Lord your God:

I Samuel 12:14

And Samuel said, Hath the Lord as great delight in burnt offerings and sacrifices, as in obeying the voice of the Lord? Behold, to obey is better than sacrifice, and to hearken than the fat of rams.

I Samuel 15:22

If ye be willing and obedient, ye shall eat the good of the land:

Isaiah 1:19

All we like sheep have gone astray; we have turned every one to his own way; and the Lord hath laid on him the iniquity of us all.

Isaiah 53:6

Not everyone that saith unto me, Lord, Lord, shall enter into the kingdom of heaven; but he that doeth the will of my Father which is in heaven.

Matthew 7:21

Jesus saith unto them, My meat is to do the will of him that sent me, and to finish his work.

John 4:34

And Jesus said unto them, I am the bread of life: he that cometh to me shall never hunger; and he that believeth on me shall never thirst.

For I came down from heaven, not to do mine own will, but the will of him that sent me.

John 6:35, 38

If ye keep my commandments, ye shall abide in my love; even as I have kept my Father's commandments, and abide in his love.

John 15:10

Go, stand and speak in the temple to the people all the words of this life.

And we are his witnesses of these things; and so is also the Holy Ghost, whom God hath given to them that obey him.

Acts 5:20, 32

For as by one man's disobedience many were made sinners, so by the obedience of one shall many be made righteous.

Romans 5:19

Though he were a Son, yet learned he obedience by the things which he suffered;

Then said he, Lo, I come to do thy will, O God. He taketh away the first, that he may establish the second.

Hebrews 5:8, 10:9

By faith Noah, being warned of God of things not seen as yet, moved with fear, prepared an ark to the saving of his house; by the which he condemned the world, and became heir of the righteousness which is by faith.

By faith Abraham, when he was called to go out into a place which he should after receive for an inheritance, obeyed; and he went out, not knowing whither he went.

Hebrews 11:7, 8

And whatsoever we ask, we receive of him, because we keep his commandments, and do those things that are pleasing in his sight.

I John 3:22

Now we know that God heareth not sinners: but if any man be a worshipper of God, and doeth his will, him he heareth.

John 9:31

Sincerity

But if from thence thou shalt seek the Lord thy God, thou shalt find him, if thou seek him with all thy heart and with all thy soul.

Deuteronomy 4:29

Hear the right, O Lord, attend unto my cry, give ear unto my prayer, that goeth not out of feigned lips.

Let my sentence come forth from thy presence; let thine eyes behold the things that are equal.

Psalm 17:1, 2

And ye shall seek me, and find me, when ye shall search for me with all your heart.

Jeremiah 29:13

But the hour cometh, and now is, when the true worshippers shall worship the Father in spirit and in truth: for the Father seeketh such to worship him.

John 4:23

Therefore let us keep the feast, not with leaven, neither with the leaven of malice and wickedness; but with the unleavened bread of sincerity and truth.

I Corinthians 5:8

And this I pray, that your love may abound yet more and more in knowledge and in all judgment;

That ye may approve things that are excellent; that ye may be sincere and without offence till the day of Christ;

Philippians 1:9, 10

Humility

And now, O Lord my God, thou hast made thy servant king instead of David my father: and I am but a little child: I know not how to go out or come in.

I Kings 3:7

If my people, which are called by my name, shall humble themselves, and pray, and seek my face, and turn from their wicked ways; then will I hear from heaven, and will forgive their sin, and will heal their land.

II Chronicles 7:14

Lord, thou hast heard the desire of the humble: thou wilt prepare their heart, thou wilt cause thine ear to hear:

Psalm 10:17

For thus saith the high and lofty One that inhabiteth eternity, whose name is Holy; I dwell in the high and holy place, with him also that is of a contrite and humble spirit, to revive the spirit of the humble, and to revive the heart of the contrite ones.

Isaiah 57:15

The centurion answered and said, Lord, I am not worthy that thou shouldest come under my roof: but speak the word only, and my servant shall be healed.

Matthew 8:8

Humble yourselves in the sight of the Lord, and he shall lift you up.

James 4:10

Purity

Thou shalt call, and I will answer thee: thou wilt have a desire to the work of thine hands.

For now thou numberest my steps: dost thou not watch over my sin?

My transgression is sealed up in a bag, and thou sewest up mine iniquity.

Job 14:15-17

I cried unto the Lord with my voice, and he heard me out of his holy hill. Selah.

Psalm 3:4

Lead me, O Lord, in thy righteousness because of mine enemies; make thy way straight before my face.

Psalm 5:8

Keep back thy servant also from presumptuous sins; let them not have dominion over me: then shall I be upright, and I shall be innocent from the great transgression.

Let the words of my mouth, and the meditation of my heart, be acceptable in thy sight, O LORD, my strength, and my redeemer.

Psalm 19:13, 14

The earth is the Lord's, and the fulness thereof; the world, and they that dwell therein.

For he hath founded it upon the seas, and established it upon the floods.

Who shall ascend into the hill of the Lord? or who shall stand in his holy place?

He that hath clean hands, and a pure heart; who hath not lifted up his soul unto vanity, nor sworn deceitfully.

He shall receive the blessing from the Lord, and righteousness from the God of his salvation.

This is the generation of them that seek him, that seek thy face, O Jacob. Selah.

Psalm 24:1-6

Judge me, O Lord; for I have walked in mine integrity: I have trusted also in the Lord; therefore I shall not slide.

Examine me, O Lord, and prove me; try my reins and my heart.

Psalm 26:1, 2

Create in me a clean heart, O God; and renew a right spirit within me.

Psalm 51:10

If I regard iniquity in my heart, the Lord will not hear me:

But verily God hath heard me; he hath attended to the voice of my prayer.

Psalm 66:18, 19

Search me, O God, and know my heart: try me, and know my thoughts:

And see if there be any wicked way in me, and lead me in the way everlasting.

Psalm 139:23, 24

The Lord is far from the wicked: but he heareth the prayer of the righteous.

Proverbs 15:29

Then said I, Woe is me! for I am undone; because I am a man of unclean lips, and I dwell in the midst of a people of unclean lips: for mine eyes have seen the King, the Lord of hosts.

Isaiah 6:5

But let man and beast be covered with sackcloth, and cry mightily unto God: yea, let them turn every one from his evil way, and from the violence that is in their hands.

Jonah 3:8

That he would grant unto us, that we being delivered out of the hand of our enemies might serve him without fear,

In holiness and righteousness before him, all the days of our life.

Luke 1:74, 75

Having therefore these promises, dearly beloved, let us cleanse ourselves from all filthiness of the flesh and spirit, perfecting holiness in the fear of God.

II Corinthians 7:1

For the eyes of the Lord are over the righteous, and his ears are open unto their prayers: but the face of the Lord is against them that do evil.

I Peter 3:12

The Lord is far from the wicked: but he heareth the prayer of the righteous.

Proverbs 15:29

Joy

But rejoice, inasmuch as ye are partakers of Christ's sufferings; that, when his glory shall be revealed, ye may be glad also with exceeding joy.

I Peter 4:13

Now unto him that is able to keep you from falling, and to present you faultless before the presence of his glory with exceeding joy.

Jude 24

The king shall joy in thy strength, O LORD; and in thy salvation how greatly shall he rejoice!

Thou hast given him his heart's desire, and hast not withholden the request of his lips. Selah.

Psalm 21:1-2

And my soul shall be joyful in the LORD: it shall rejoice in his salvation.

Psalm 35:9

Let them shout for joy, and be glad, that favour my righteous cause: yea, let them say continually, Let the Lord be magnified, which hath pleasure in the prosperity of his servant.

And my tongue shall speak of thy righteousness and of thy praise all the day long.

Psalm 35:27-28

Create in me a clean heart, O God; and renew a right spirit within me.

Cast me not away from thy presence; and take not thy holy spirit from me.

Restore unto me the joy of thy salvation; and uphold me with thy free spirit.

Then will I teach transgressors thy ways; and sinners shall be converted unto thee.

Psalm 51:10-13

Conditions for Prayer

Praying in the Word

My son, attend to my words; incline thine ear unto my sayings.

Let them not depart from thine eyes; keep them in the midst of thine heart.

For they are life unto those that find them, and health to all their flesh.

Keep thy heart with all diligence; for out of it are the issues of life.

Proverbs 4:20-23

Thy words were found, and I did eat them; and thy word was unto me the joy and rejoicing of mine heart: for I am called by thy name, O Lord God of hosts.

Jeremiah 15:16

The centurion answered and said, Lord, I am not worthy that thou shouldest come under my roof: but speak the word only, and my servant shall be healed.

Matthew 8:8

If ye abide in me, and my words abide in you, ye shall ask what ye will, and it shall be done unto you.

John 15:7

And for their sakes I sanctify myself, that they also might be sanctified through the truth.

Neither pray I for these alone, but for them also which shall believe on me through their word;

John 17:19, 20

But we will give ourselves continually to prayer, and to the ministry of the word.

Acts 6:4

Finally, brethren, pray for us, that the word of the Lord may have free course, and be glorified, even as it is with you:

II Thessalonians 3:1

For every creature of God is good, and nothing to be refused if it be received with thanksgiving.

For it is sanctified by the word of God and prayer.

I Timothy 4:4, 5

If any man will do his will, he shall know of the doctrine, whether it be of God, or whether I speak of myself.

John 7:17

And they prayed, and said, Thou, Lord, which knowest the hearts of all men, shew whether of these two thou hast chosen.

Acts 1:24

And when he would not be persuaded, we ceased, saying, The will of the Lord be done.

Acts 21:14

And be not conformed to this world: but be ye transformed by the renewing of your mind, that ye may prove what is that good, and acceptable, and perfect, will of God.

Romans 12:2

Wherefore be ye not unwise, but understanding what the will of the Lord is.

Ephesians 5:17

For this cause we also, since the day we heard it, do not cease to pray for you, and to desire that ye might be filled with the knowledge of his will in all wisdom and spiritual understanding.

Colossians 1:9

And this is the confidence that we have in him, that, if we ask any thing according to his will, he heareth us:

I John 5:14

And he preached in their synagogues throughout all Galilee, and cast out devils.

And there came a leper to him, beseeching him, and kneeling down to him, and saying unto him, If thou wilt, thou canst make me clean.

And Jesus, moved with compassion, put forth his hand, and touched him, and saith unto him, I will; be thou clean.

And as soon as he had spoken, immediately the leprosy departed from him, and he was cleansed.

Mark 1:39-42

Jesus saith unto them, My meat is to do the will of him that sent me, and to finish his work.

John 4:34

Praying in Faith

Now faith is the substance of things hoped for, the evidence of things not seen.

For by it the elders obtained a good report.

Through faith we understand that the worlds were framed by the word of God, so that things which are seen were not made of things which do appear.

By faith Abel offered unto God a more excellent sacrifice than Cain, by which he obtained witness that he was righteous, God testifying of his gifts: and by it he being dead yet speaketh.

By faith Enoch was translated that he should not see death; and was not found, because God had translated him: for before his translation he had this testimony, that he pleased God.

But without faith it is impossible to please him; for he that cometh to God must believe that he is, and that he is a rewarder of them that diligently seek him.

By faith Noah, being warned of God of things not seen as yet, moved with fear, prepared an ark to the saving of his house; by the which he condemned the world, and became heir of the righteousness which is by faith.

By faith Abraham, when he was called to go out into a place which he should after receive for an inheritance, obeyed; and he went out, not knowing whither he went.

By faith he sojourned in the land of promise, as in a strange country, dwelling in tabernacles with Isaac and Jacob, the heirs with him of the same promise:

For he looked for a city which hath foundations, whose builder and maker is God.

Through faith also Sara herself received strength to conceive seed, and was delivered of a child when she was past age, because she judged him faithful who had promised.

Therefore sprang there even of one, and him as good as dead, so many as the stars of the sky in multitude, and as the sand which is by the sea shore innumerable.

These all died in faith, not having received the promises, but having seen them afar off, and were persuaded of them, and embraced them, and confessed that they were strangers and pilgrims on the earth.

For they that say such things declare plainly that they seek a country.

And truly, if they had been mindful of that country from whence they came out, they might have had opportunity to have returned.

But now they desire a better country, that is, an heavenly: wherefore God is not ashamed to be called their God: for he hath prepared for them a city.

By faith Abraham, when he was tried, offered up Isaac; and he that had received the promises offered up his only begotten son,

Of whom it was said, That in Isaac shall thy seed be called.

Accounting that God was able to raise him up, even from the dead; from whence also he received him in a figure.

By faith Isaac blessed Jacob and Esau concerning things to come.

By faith Jacob, when he was a-dying, blessed both the sons of Joseph; and worshipped, leaning upon the top of his staff.

By faith Joseph, when he died, made mention of the departing of the children of Israel; and gave commandment concerning his bones.

By faith Moses, when he was born, was hid three months of his parents, because they saw he was a proper child; and they were not afraid of the king's commandment.

By faith Moses, when he was come to years, refused to be called the son of Pharaoh's daughter;

Choosing rather to suffer affliction with the people of God, than to enjoy the pleasures of sin for a season;

Esteeming the reproach of Christ greater riches than the treasures in Egypt: for he had respect unto the recompence of the reward.

By faith he forsook Egypt, not fearing the wrath of the king: for he endured, as seeing him who is invisible.

Through faith he kept the passover, and the sprinkling of blood, lest he that destroyed the firstborn should touch them.

By faith they passed through the Red sea as by dry land: which the Egyptians assaying to do were drowned.

By faith the walls of Jericho fell down, after they were compassed about seven days.

By faith the harlot Rahab perished not with them that believed not, when she had received the spies with peace.

And what shall I more say? for the time would fail me to tell of Gedeon, and of Barak, and of Sampson, and of Jephthae; of David also, and Samuel, and of the prophets:

Who through faith subdued kingdoms, wrought righteousness, obtained promises, stopped the mouths of lions,

Quenched the violence of fire, escaped the edge of the sword, out of weakness were made strong, waxed valiant in fight, turned to flight the armies of the aliens.

Women received their dead raised to life again: and others were tortured, not accepting deliverance; that they might obtain a better resurrection:

And others had trial of cruel mockings and scourgings, yea, moreover of bonds and imprisonment:

They were stoned, they were sawn asunder, were tempted, were slain with the sword: they wandered about in sheepskins and goatskins; being destitute, afflicted, tormented;

(Of whom the world was not worthy:) they wandered in deserts, and in mountains, and in dens and caves of the earth.

And these all, having obtained a good report through faith, received not the promise:

God having provided some better thing for us, that they without us should not be made perfect.

Hebrews 11:1-40

And when they were come to the multitude, there came to him a certain man, kneeling down to him, and saying,

Lord, have mercy on my son: for he is lunatic, and sore vexed: for oftimes he falleth into the fire, and oft into the water.

And I brought him to thy disciples, and they could not cure him.

Then Jesus answered and said, O faithless and perverse generation, how long shall I be with you? how long shall I suffer you? bring him hither to me.

And Jesus rebuked the devil; and he departed out of him: and the child was cured from that very hour.

Then came the disciples to Jesus apart, and said, Why could not we cast him out?

And Jesus said unto them, Because of your unbelief: for verily I say unto you, If ye have faith as a grain of mustard seed ye shall say unto this mountain, Remove hence to yonder place and it shall remove; and nothing shall be impossible unto you.

Matthew 17:14-20

Now in the morning as he returned into the city, he hungered.

And when he saw a fig tree in the way, he came to it, and found nothing thereon, but leaves only, and said unto it, Let no fruit grow on thee henceforward for ever. And presently the fig tree withered away.

And when the disciples saw it, they marvelled, saying, How soon is the fig tree withered away!

Jesus answered and said unto them, Verily I say unto you, If ye have faith, and doubt not, ye shall not only do this which is done to the fig tree, but also if ye shall say unto this mountain, Be thou removed, and be thou cast into the sea; it shall be done.

Matthew 21:18-21

If then God so clothe the grass, which is today in the field, and to-morrow is cast into the oven; how much more will he clothe you, O ye of little faith?

Luke 12:28

By whom also we have access by faith into this grace wherein we stand, and rejoice in hope of the glory of God.

Romans 5:2

That ye be not slothful, but followers of them who through faith and patience inherit the promises.

Hebrews 6:12

And, behold, a woman, which was diseased with an issue of blood twelve years, came behind him, and touched the hem of his garment:

For she said within herself, If I may but touch his garment, I shall be whole.

But Jesus turned him about, and when he saw her, he said, Daughter, be of good comfort; thy faith hath made thee whole. And the woman was made whole from that hour.

And when Jesus came into the ruler's house, and saw the minstrels and the people making a noise,

He said unto them, Give place: for the maid is not dead, but sleepeth. And they laughed him to scorn.

But when the people were put forth, he went in, and took her by the hand, and the maid arose.

And the fame hereof went abroad into all that land.

Matthew 9:20-26

And immediately Jesus stretched forth his hand, and caught him, and said unto him, O thou of little faith, wherefore didst thou doubt?

And he besought him that they might only

touch the hem of his garment: and as many as touched were made perfectly whole.

Matthew 14:31, 36

Then Jesus answered and said unto her, O woman, great is thy faith: be it unto thee even as thou wilt. And her daughter was made whole from that very hour. *Matthew 15:28*

And Jesus answering saith unto them, Have faith in God.

For verily I say unto you, That whosoever shall say unto this mountain, Be thou removed, and be thou cast into the sea; and shall not doubt in his heart, but shall believe that those things which he saith shall come to pass; he shall have whatsoever he saith.

Therefore I say unto you, What things soever ye desire, when ye pray, believe that ye receive them, and ye shall have them.

Mark 11:22-24

And the apostles said unto the Lord, Increase our faith. *Luke 17:5*

For therein is the righteousness of God revealed from faith to faith: as it is written, The just shall live by faith. *Romans 1:17*

He staggered not at the promise of God through unbelief; but was strong in faith, giving glory to God;

And being fully persuaded that, what he had promised, he was able also to perform.

Romans 4:20-21

So then faith cometh by hearing, and hearing by the word of God.

Romans 10:17

And he that doubteth is damned if he eat, because he eateth not of faith: for whatsoever is not of faith is sin.

Romans 14:23

While we look not at the things which are seen, but at the things which are not seen: for the things which are seen are temporal; but the things which are not seen are eternal.

II Corinthians 4:18

For in Jesus Christ neither circumcision availeth any thing, nor uncircumcision; but faith which worketh by love.

Galations 5:6

For this cause also thank we God without ceasing, because, when ye received the word of God which ye heard of us, ye received it not as the word of men, but as it is in truth, the word of God, which effectually worketh also in you that believe.

I Thessalonians 2:13

But let him ask in faith, nothing wavering. For he that wavereth is like a wave of the sea driven with the wind and tossed.

For let not that man think that he shall receive any thing of the Lord.

James 1:6, 7

And the prayer of faith shall save the sick, and the Lord shall raise him up; and if he have commited sins, they shall be forgiven him.

James 5:15

For whatsoever is born of God overcometh the world: and this is the victory that overcometh the world, even our faith.

I John 5:4

By whom also we have access by faith into this grace wherein we stand, and rejoice in hope of the glory of God.

Romans 5:2

For through him we both have access by one Spirit unto the Father.

Ephesians 2:18

Which in other ages was not made known unto the sons of men, as it is now revealed unto his holy apostles and prophets by the Spirit;

That the Gentiles should be fellow-heirs, and of the same body and partakers of his promise in Christ by the gospel:

Whereof I was made a minister, according to the gift of the grace of God given unto me by the effectual working of his power.

Unto me, who am less than the least of all saints, is this grace given, that I should preach among the Gentiles the unsearchable riches of Christ;

And to make all men see what is the fellowship of the mystery, which from the beginning of the world hath been hid in God, who created all things by Jesus Christ:

To the intent that now unto the principalities and powers in heavenly places might be known by the church the manifold wisdom of God,

According to the eternal purpose which he purposed in Christ Jesus our Lord:

In whom we have boldness and access with confidence by the faith of him.

Ephesians 3:5-12

Having therefore, brethren, boldness to enter into the holiest by the blood of Jesus,

By a new and living way, which he hath consecrated for us, through the veil, that is to say, his flesh;

And having an high priest over the house of God;

Let us draw near with a true heart in full assurance of faith, having our hearts sprinkled from an evil conscience, and our bodies washed with pure water.

Let us hold fast the profession of our faith without wavering; (for he is faithful that promised;)

Hebrews 10:19-23

Praying in the Spirit

For if I pray in an unknown tongue, my spirit prayeth, but my understanding is unfruitful.

What is it then? I will pray with the spirit, and I will pray with the understanding also: I will sing with the spirit, and I will sing with the understanding also.

I Corinthians 14:14, 15

Praying always with all prayer and supplication in the Spirit, and watching thereunto with all perseverance and supplication for all saints;

Ephesians 6:18

But ye, beloved, building up yourselves on your most holy faith, praying in the Holy Ghost,

Keep yourselves in the love of God, looking for the mercy of our Lord Jesus Christ unto eternal life.

Jude 1:20-21

Howbeit when he, the Spirit of truth, is come, he will guide you into all truth: for he shall not speak of himself; but whatsoever he shall hear, that shall he speak: and he will shew you things to come.

John 16:13

Likewise the Spirit also helpeth our infirmities: for we know not what we should pray for as we ought: but the Spirit itself maketh intercession for us with groanings which cannot be uttered.

And he that searcheth the hearts knoweth what is the mind of the Spirit, because he maketh intercession for the saints according to the will of God.

Romans 8:26-27

Hindrances to Prayer

Then ye answered and said unto me, We have sinned against the LORD, we will go up and fight according to all that the LORD our God commanded us. And when ye had girded on every man his weapons of war, ye were ready to go up into the hill.

And the LORD said unto me, Say unto them, Go not up, neither fight; for I am not among you; lest ye be smitten before your enemies.

So I spake unto you; and ye would not hear, but rebelled against the commandment of the LORD, and went presumptuously up into the hill.

And the Amorites, which dwelt in that mountain, came out against you, and chased you, as bees do, and destroyed you in Seir, even unto Hormah.

And ye returned and wept before the LORD; but the LORD would not hearken to your voice, nor give ear unto you.

Deuteronomy 1:41-45

But the Lord was wroth with me for your sakes, and would not hear me: and the Lord said unto me, Let it suffice thee; speak no more unto me of this matter.

Deuteronomy 3:26

And Joshua rent his clothes, and fell to the earth upon his face before the ark of the Lord until eventide, he and the elders of Israel, and put dust upon their heads.

And Joshua said, Alas, O Lord God, wherefore hast thou at all brought this people over Jordan, to deliver us into the land of the Amorites, to destroy us? would to God we had been content, and dwelt on the other side of Jordan!

O Lord, what shall I say, when Israel turneth their backs before their enemies!

For the Canaanites and all the inhabitants of the land shall hear of it, and shall environ us round, and cut off our name from the earth: and what wilt thou do unto thy great name?

Joshua 7:6-9

There they cry, but none giveth answer, because of the pride of evil men.

Surely God will not hear vanity, neither will the Almighty regard it.

Job 35:12, 13

If I regard iniquity in my heart, the Lord will not hear me.

Psalm 66:18

Because I have called, and ye refused; I have stretched out my hand, and no man regarded;

But ye have set at nought all my counsel, and would none of my reproof:

I also will laugh at your calamity; I will mock when your fear cometh;

When your fear cometh as desolation, and your destruction cometh as a whirlwind; when distress and anguish cometh upon you.

Then shall they call upon me, but I will not answer; they shall seek me early, but they shall not find me:

For that they hated knowledge, and did not choose the fear of the Lord:

They would none of my counsel: they despised all my reproof.

Proverbs 1:24-30

The sacrifice of the wicked is an abomination to the Lord: but the prayer of the upright is his delight.

Proverbs 15:8

Whoso stoppeth his ears at the cry of the poor, he also shall cry himself, but shall not be heard.

Proverbs 21:13

He that turneth away his ear from hearing the law, even his prayer shall be an abomination.

Proverbs 28:9

And when ye spread forth your hands, I will hide mine eyes from you: yea, when ye make many prayers, I will not hear: your hands are full of blood.

Isaiah 1:15

Behold, the Lord's hand is not shortened, that is cannot save; neither his ear heavy, that it cannot hear:

But your iniquities have separated between you and your God, and your sins have hid his face from you, that he will not hear.

Isaiah 59:1, 2

Therefore thus saith the Lord, Behold, I will bring evil upon them, which they shall not be able to escape; and though they shall cry unto me, I will not hearken unto them.

Jeremiah 11:11

Then said the Lord unto me, Though Moses and Samuel stood before me, yet my mind could not be toward this people: cast them out of my sight, and let them go forth.

Jeremiah 15:1

Also when I cry and shout, he shutteth out my prayer.

Thou hast covered thyself with a cloud, that our prayer should not pass through.

Lamentations 3:8, 44

Then came certain of the elders of Israel unto me, and sat before me.

And the word of the Lord came unto me, saying,

Son of man, these men have set up their idols in their heart, and put the stumblingblock of their iniquity before their face: should I be inquired of at all by them?

Ezekiel 14:1-3

Then they shall cry unto the Lord, but he will not hear them: he will even hide his face from them at that time, as they have behaved themselves ill in their doings.

Micah 3:4

But they refused to hearken, and pulled away the shoulder, and stopped their ears, that they should not hear.

Yea, they made their hearts as an adamant stone, lest they should hear the law, and the words which the Lord of hosts hath sent in his spirit by the former prophets: therefore came a great wrath from the Lord of hosts.

Therefore it is come to pass, that as he cried, and they would not hear; so they cried, and I would not hear, saith the Lord of hosts:

Zechariah 7:11-13

They shall go with their flocks and with their herds to seek the Lord; but they shall not find him; he hath withdrawn himself from them.

Hosea 5:6

Now I pray to God that ye do no evil; not that we should appear approved, but that ye should do that which is honest, though we be as reprobates.

II Corinthians 13:7

Ye lust, and have not: ye kill, and desire to have, and cannot obtain: ye fight and war, yet ye have not, because ye ask not.

Ye ask, and receive not, because ye ask amiss, that ye may consume it upon your lusts.

James 4:2-3

Likewise, ye husbands, dwell with them according to knowledge, giving honour unto the wife, as unto the weaker vessel, and as being heirs together of the grace of life; that your prayers be not hindered.

For the eyes of the Lord are over the righteous, and his ears are open unto their prayers: but the face of the Lord is against them that do evil.

I Peter 3:7, 12

Spiritual Warfare Through Prayer

Authority in the Name of Jesus

Let the word of Christ dwell in you richly in all wisdom; teaching and admonishing one another in psalms and hymns and spiritual songs, singing with grace in your hearts to the Lord.

And whatsoever ye do in word or deed, do all in the name of the Lord Jesus, giving thanks to God and the Father by him.

Colossians 3:16-17

And in that day ye shall ask me nothing. Verily, verily, I say unto you, Whatsoever ye shall ask the Father in my name, he will give it you.

Hitherto have ye asked nothing in my name: ask, and ye shall receive, that your joy may be full.

John 16:23, 24

If ye abide in me, and my words abide in you, ye shall ask what ye will, and it shall be done unto you.

Herein is my Father glorified, that ye bear much fruit; so shall ye be my disciples.

As the Father hath loved me, so have I loved you: continue ye in my love.

If ye keep my commandments, ye shall abide in my love; even as I have kept my Father's commandments, and abide in his love.

Ye have not chosen me, but I have chosen you, and ordained you, that ye should go and bring forth fruit, and that your fruit should remain: that whatsoever ye shall ask of the Father in my name, he may give it to you.

John 15:7-10, 16

For if our heart condemn us, God is greater than our heart, and knoweth all things.

Beloved, if our heart condemn us not, then have we confidence toward God.

And whatsoever we ask, we receive of him, because we keep his commandments, and do those things that are pleasing in his sight.

I John 3:20-22

And this is the confidence that we have in him, that, if we ask anything according to his will, he heareth us:

And if we know that he hear us, whatsoever we ask, we know that we have the petitions that we desired of him.

I John 5:14-15

And Jesus said unto them, Because of your unbelief: for verily I say unto you, If ye have faith as a grain of mustard seed, ye shall say unto this mountain, Remove hence to yonder place; and it shall remove; and nothing shall be impossible unto you.

Howbeit this kind goeth not out but by prayer and fasting.

And while they abode in Galilee, Jesus said unto them, The Son of man shall be betrayed into the hands of men:

And they shall kill him, and the third day he shall be raised again. And they were exceeding sorry.

Matthew 17:20-23

And I will bring the third part through the fire, and will refine them as silver is refined, and will try them as gold is tried: they shall call on my name, and I will hear them: I will say, It is my people: and they shall say, The Lord is my God.

Zechariah 13:9

Again I say unto you, That if two of you shall agree on earth as touching any thing that they shall ask, it shall be done for them of my Father which is in heaven.

For where two or three are gathered together in my name, there am I in the midst of them.

Matthew 18:19-20

And these signs shall follow them that believe; In my name shall they cast out devils; they shall speak with new tongues;

Mark 16:17

Verily, verily, I say unto you, He that believeth on me, the works that I do shall he do also; and greater works than these shall he do; because I go unto my Father.

And whatsoever ye shall ask in my name, that will I do, that the Father may be glorified in the Son.

If ye shall ask any thing in my name, I will do it.

John 14:12-14

Persistance and Prevailing In Prayer

And Jacob was left alone; and there wrestled a man with him until the breaking of the day.

And when he saw that he prevailed not against him, he touched the hollow of his thigh; and the hollow of Jacob's thigh was out of joint, as he wrestled with him.

And he said, Let me go, for the day breaketh. And he said, I will not let thee go, except thou bless me.

Genesis 32:24-26

Blessed be the Lord my strength, which teacheth my hands to war, and my fingers to fight:
Psalm 144:1

Put on the whole armour of God, that ye may be able to stand against the wiles of the devil.

For we wrestle not against flesh and blood, but against principalities, against powers, against the rulers of the darkness of this world, against spiritual wickedness in high places.

Ephesians 6:11-12

So Ahab went up to eat and drink. And Elijah went up to the top of Carmel; and he cast himself down upon the earth, and put his face between his knees,

And said to his servant, Go up now, look toward the sea. And he went up, and looked, and said, There is nothing. And he said, Go again seven times.

And it came to pass at the seventh time, that he said, Behold, there ariseth a little cloud out of the sea, like a man's hand. And he said, Go up, say unto Ahab, Prepare thy chariot, and get thee down, that the rain stop thee not.

And it came to pass in the mean while, that the heaven was black with clouds and wind, and there was a great rain. And Ahab rode, and went to Jezreel.

I Kings 18:42-45

Seek the Lord and his strength seek his face continually.

I Chronicles 16:11

And, behold, a woman of Canaan came out of the same coasts, and cried unto him, saying, Have mercy on me, O Lord, thou son of David; my daughter is grievously vexed with a devil.

But he answered her not a word. And his disciples came and besought him, saying, Send her away; for she crieth after us.

But he answered and said, I am not sent but unto the lost sheep of the house of Israel.

Then came she and worshipped him, saying, Lord, help me.

But he answered and said, It is not meet to take the children's bread, and to cast it to dogs.

And she said, Truth, Lord: yet the dogs eat of the crumbs which fall from their master's table.

Then Jesus answered and said unto her, O woman, great is thy faith: be it unto thee even as thou wilt. And her daughter was made whole from that very hour.

Matthew 15:22-28

And it came to pass in those days, that he went out into a mountain to pray, and continued all night in prayer to God.

Luke 6:12

And he said unto them, Which of you shall have a friend, and shall go unto him at midnight, and say unto him, Friend, lend me three loaves:

For a friend of mine in his journey is come to me, and I have nothing to set before him?

And he from within shall answer and say, Trouble me not: the door is now shut, and my children are with me in bed; I cannot rise and give thee.

I say unto you, Though he will not rise and give him, because he is his friend, yet because of his importunity he will rise and give him as many as he needeth.

And I say unto you, Ask, and it shall be given you; seek, and ye shall find; knock, and it shall be opened unto you.

For every one that asketh receiveth; and he that seeketh findeth; and to him that knocketh it shall be opened.

Luke 11:5-10

And he spake a parable unto them to this end, that men ought always to pray, and not to faint;

Saying, There was in a city a judge, which feared not God, neither regarded man:

And there was a widow in that city; and she came unto him, saying, Avenge me of mine adversary.

And he would not for a while; but afterward he said within himself, Though I fear not God, nor regard man;

Yet because this widow troubleth me, I will avenge her, lest by her continual coming she weary me.

And the Lord said, Hear what the unjust judge saith.

And shall not God avenge his own elect, which cry day and night unto him, though he bear long with them?

Luke 18:1-7

And being in an agony he prayed more earnestly: and his sweat was as it were great drops of blood falling down to the ground.

Luke 22:44

These all continued with one accord in prayer and supplication, with the women, and Mary the mother of Jesus, and with his brethren.

Acts 1:14

Then they that gladly received his word were baptized: and the same day there were added unto them about three thousand souls.

And they continued stedfastly in the apostles' doctrine and fellowship, and in breaking of bread, and in prayers.

Acts 2:41, 42

Praying always with all prayer and supplication in the Spirit, and watching thereunto with all perseverance and supplication for all saints;

And for me, that utterance may be given unto me, that I may open my mouth boldly, to make known the mystery of the gospel,

For which I am an ambassador in bonds: that therein I may speak boldly, as I ought to speak.

Ephesians 6:18-20

Continue in prayer, and watch in the same with thanksgiving;

Withal praying also for us, that God would open unto us a door of utterance, to speak the mystery of Christ, for which I am also in bonds:
Colossians 4:2-3

My friends scorn me: but mine eye poureth out tears unto God.
Job 16:20

I am weary with my groaning; all the night make I my bed to swim; I water my couch with my tears.
Psalm 6:6

For his anger endureth but a moment; in his favour is life: weeping may endure for a night, but joy cometh in the morning.

Psalm 30:5

Thou tellest my wanderings: put thou my tears into thy bottle: are they not in thy book?
When I cry unto thee, then shall mine enemies turn back: this I know; for God is for me.
In God will I praise his word: in the Lord will I praise his word.
Psalm 56:8-10

They that sow in tears shall reap in joy.
Psalm 126:5

Oh that my head were waters, and mine eyes a fountain of tears, that I might weep day and night for the slain of the daughter of my people!

Jeremiah 9:1

Jesus said unto him, If thou believe, all things are possible to him that believeth.

And straightway the father of the child cried out, and said with tears, Lord, I believe; help thou mine unbelief.

Mark 9:23, 24

Blessed are ye that hunger now: for ye shall be filled. Blessed are ye that weep now: for ye shall laugh.

Luke 6:21

Now there was at Joppa a certain disciple named Tabitha, which by interpretation is called Dorcas: this woman was full of good works and almsdeeds which she did.

And it came to pass in those days, that she was sick, and died: whom when they had washed, they laid her in an upper chamber.

And forasmuch as Lydda was nigh to Joppa, and the disciples had heard that Peter was there, they sent unto him two men, desiring him that he would not delay to come to them.

Then Peter arose and went with them. When he was come, they brought him into the upper chamber: and all the widows stood by him weeping, and shewing the coats and garments which Dorcas made, while she was with them.

Acts 9:36-39

Let integrity and uprightness preserve me; for I wait on thee.

Psalm 25:21

Wait on the Lord: be of good courage, and he shall strengthen thine heart: wait, I say, on the Lord.

Psalm 27:14

I waited patiently for the Lord; and he inclined unto me, and heard my cry.

Psalm 40:1

I wait for the Lord, my soul doth wait, and in his word do I hope.

Psalm 130:5

But they that wait upon the Lord shall renew their strength; they shall mount up with wings as eagles; they shall run, and not be weary; and they shall walk, and not faint.

Isaiah 40:31

Therefore I will look unto the Lord; I will wait for the God of my salvation: my God will hear me.

Micah 7:7

Nevertheless we made our prayer unto our God, and set a watch against them day and night, because of them.

Nehemiah 4:9

Watch and pray, that ye enter not into temptation: the spirit indeed is willing, but the flesh is weak.

Matthew 26:41

Watch ye therefore, and pray always, that ye may be accounted worthy to escape all these things that shall come to pass, and to stand before the Son of man.

Luke 21:36

Continue in prayer, and watch in the same with thanksgiving;

Colossians 4:2

But the end of all things is at hand: be ye therefore sober, and watch unto prayer.

I Peter 4:7

And there is none that calleth upon thy name, that stirreth up himself to take hold of thee: for thou hast hid thy face from us, and hast consumed us, because of our iniquities.

Isaiah 64:7

And when thou prayest, thou shalt not be as the hypocrites are: for they love to pray standing in the synagogues and in the corners of the streets, that they may be seen of men. Verily I say unto you, They have their reward.

But thou, when thou prayest, enter into thy closet, and when thou hast shut thy door, pray to thy Father which is in secret; and thy Father which seeth in secret shall reward thee openly.

But when ye pray, use not vain repetitions, as the heathen do: for they think that they shall be heard for their much speaking.

Be not ye therefore like unto them: for your Father knoweth what things ye have need of before ye ask him.

Matthew 6:5-8

Jesus answered and said unto them, Verily I say unto you, If ye have faith, and doubt not, ye shall not only do this which is done to the fig tree, but also if ye shall say unto this mountain, Be thou removed, and be thou cast into the sea; it shall be done.

And all things, whatsoever ye shall ask in prayer, believing, ye shall receive.

Matthew 21:21, 22

Therefore I say unto you, What things soever ye desire, when ye pray, believe that ye receive them, and ye shall have them.

Mark 11:24

Let us therefore come boldly unto the throne of grace, that we may obtain mercy, and find grace to help in time of need.

Hebrews 4:16

Petitions and Patterns For Prayer

And he spake a parable unto them to this end, that men ought always to pray, and not to faint;
Luke 18:1

For this cause we also, since the day we heard it, do not cease to pray for you, and to desire that ye might be filled with the knowledge of his will in all wisdom and spiritual understanding;
Colossians 1:9

So being affectionately desirous of you, we were willing to have imparted unto you, not the gospel of God only, but also our own souls, because ye were dear unto us.
I Thessalonians 2:8

Pray without ceasing.
In everything give thanks: for this is the will of God in Christ Jesus concerning you.
I Thessalonians 5:17, 18

Wherefore also we pray always for you, that our God would count you worthy of this calling and fulfil all the good pleasure of his goodness, and the work of faith with power:
II Thessalonians 1:11

I cried to thee, O Lord; and unto the Lord I made supplication.

Psalm 30:8

Evening, and morning, and at noon, will I pray, and cry aloud: and he shall hear my voice.

Psalm 55:17

And Moses went out of the city from Pharaoh, and spread abroad his hands unto the Lord: and the thunders and hail ceased, and the rain was not poured upon the earth.

Exodus 9:33

And the Lord said unto Moses, I will do this thing also that thou hast spoken: for thou hast found grace in my sight, and I know thee by name.

Exodus 33:17

And I besought the Lord at that time, saying, O Lord GOD, thou hast begun to shew thy servant greatness, and thy mighty hand: for what God is there in heaven or in earth, that can do according to thy works, and according to thy might?

Deuteronomy 3:23-24

In God I will praise his word, in God I have put my trust; I will not fear what flesh can do unto me.

Psalm 56:4

Remember me, O Lord, with the favour that thou bearest unto thy people: O visit me with thy salvation.

That I may see the good of thy chosen, that I may rejoice in the gladness of thy nation, that I may glory with thine inheritance.

Psalm 106:4, 5

I will offer to thee the sacrifice of thanksgiving, and will call upon the name of the Lord.

Psalm 116:17

Ask, and it shall be given you; seek, and ye shall find; knock, and it shall be opened unto you:

For every one that asketh receiveth; and he that seeketh findeth; and to him that knocketh it shall be opened.

Or what man is there of you, whom if his son ask bread, will he give him a stone?

Or if he ask a fish, will he give him a serpent?

If ye then, being evil, know how to give good gifts unto your children, how much more shall your Father which is in heaven give good things to them that ask him?

Matthew 7:7-11

Have respect therefore to the prayer of thy servant, and to his supplication, O Lord my God, to hearken unto the cry and the prayer which thy servant prayeth before thee:

II Chronicles 6:19

Only do not two things unto me: then will I not hide myself from thee.

Withdraw thine hand far from me: and let not thy dread make me afraid.

Then call thou, and I will answer: or let me speak, and answer thou me.

Job 13:20-22

So that they cause the cry of the poor to come unto him, and he heareth the cry of the afflicted.

Job 34:28

But know that the Lord hath set apart him that is godly for himself: the Lord will hear when I call unto him.

Psalm 4:3

Give ear to thy words, O Lord, consider my meditation.

Hearken unto the voice of my cry, my King, and my God: for unto thee will I pray.

My voice shalt thou hear in the morning, O Lord; in the morning will I direct my prayer unto thee, and will look up.

Psalm 5:1-3

The Lord is far from the wicked: but he heareth the prayer of the righteous.

Proverbs 15:29

Cast thy bread upon the waters: for thou shalt find it after many days.

Ecclesiastes 11:1

And I will give thee the treasures of darkness, and hidden riches of secret places, that thou mayest know that I, the Lord, which call thee by thy name, am the God of Israel.

Isaiah 45:3

Then shalt thou call, and the Lord shall answer; thou shalt cry, and he shall say, Here I am. If thou take away from the midst of thee the yoke, the putting forth of the finger, and speaking vanity;

Isaiah 58:9

Call unto me, and I will answer thee, and shew thee great and mighty things, which thou knowest not.

Jeremiah 33:3

And I will strengthen the house of Judah, and I will save the house of Joseph, and I will bring them again to place them; for I have mercy upon them: and they shall be as though I had not cast them off: for I am the Lord God, and will hear them.

Zechariah 10:6

And the man bowed down his head, and worshipped the Lord.

And I bowed down my head, and worshipped the Lord, and blessed the Lord God of my master Abraham, which had led me in the right way to take my master's brother's daughter unto his son.

And it came to pass, that, when Abraham's servant heard their words, he worshipped the Lord, bowing himself to the earth.

Genesis 24:26, 48, 52

And when thou prayest, thou shalt not be as the hypocrites are: for they love to pray standing in the synagogues and in the corners of the streets, that they may be seen of men. Verily I say unto you, They have their reward.

But thou, when thou prayest, enter into thy closet, and when thou hast shut thy door, pray to thy Father which is in secret; and thy Father which seeth in secret shall reward thee openly.

But when ye pray, use not vain repetitions, as the heathen do: for they think that they shall be heard for their much speaking.

Be not ye therefore like unto them: for your Father knoweth what things ye have need of before ye ask him.

After this manner therefore pray ye: Our Father which art in heaven, Hallowed be thy name.

Thy kingdom come. Thy will be done in earth, as it is in heaven.

Give us this day our daily bread.

And forgive us our debts, as we forgive our debtors.

And lead us not into temptation, but deliver us from evil: For thine is the kingdom and the power, and the glory, for ever. Amen.

For if ye forgive men their trespasses, your heavenly Father will also forgive you;

But if ye forgive not men their trespasses, neither will your Father forgive your trespasses.

Matthew 6:5-15

And Moses made haste, and bowed his head toward the earth, and worshipped.

Exodus 34:8

And David said to all the congregation, Now bless the Lord your God. And all the congregation blessed the Lord God of their fathers, and bowed down their heads, and worshipped the Lord, and the king.

I Chronicles 29:20

And when they had made an end of offering, the king and all that were present with him bowed themselves, and worshipped.

Moreover Hezekiah the king and the princes commanded the Levites to sing praise unto the Lord with the words of David, and of Asaph the seer. And they sang praises with gladness, and they bowed their heads and worshipped.

I Chronicles 29:29, 30

And Ezra blessed the Lord, the great God. And all the people answered, Amen, Amen, with lifting up their hands: and they bowed their heads, and worshipped the Lord with their faces to the ground.

Nehemiah 8:6

And David the king came and sat before the Lord, and said, Who am I, O Lord God, and what is mine house, that thou hast brought me hitherto?

I Chronicles 17:16

And suddenly there came a sound from heaven as of a rushing mighty wind, and it filled all the house where they were sitting.

Acts 2:2

And it was so, that when Solomon had made an end of praying all this prayer and supplication unto the Lord, he arose from before the altar of the Lord, from kneeling on his knees with his hands spread up to heaven.

I Kings 8:54

For Solomon had made a brasen scaffold, of five cubits long, and five cubits broad, and three cubits high, and had set it in the midst of the court: and upon it he stood, and kneeled down upon his knees before all the congregation of Israel, and spread forth his hands toward heaven.

II Chronicles 6:13

And when he had thus spoken, he kneeled down, and prayed with them all.

Acts 20:36

And Abram fell on his face: and God talked with him, saying,

As for me, behold, my covenant is with thee, and thou shalt be a father of many nations.

Genesis 17:3-4

And Jehoshaphat bowed his head with his face to the ground: and all Judah and the inhabitants of Jerusalem fell before the Lord, worshipping the LORD.

II Chronicles 20:18

Now when Ezra had prayed, and when he had confessed, weeping and casting himself down before the house of God, there assembled unto him out of Israel a very great congregation of men and women and children: for the people wept very sore.

Ezra 10:1

As the appearance of the bow that is in the cloud in the day of rain, so was the appearance of the brightness round about. This was the appearance of the likeness of the glory of the Lord. And when I saw it, I fell upon my face, and I heard a voice of one that spake.

Ezekiel 1:28

Yet heard I the voice of his words: and when I heard the voice of his words, then was I in a deep sleep on my face, and my face toward the ground.

Daniel 10:9

And when the disciples heard it, they fell on their face, and were sore afraid.

Matthew 17:6

On the morrow, as they went on their journey, and drew nigh unto the city, Peter went up upon the housetop to pray about the sixth hour:

And he became very hungry, and would have eaten: but while they made ready, he fell into a trance,

Acts 10:9, 10

And when I saw him, I fell at his feet as dead. And he laid his right hand upon me, saying unto me, Fear not; I am the first and the last:

Revelation 1:17

And the king turned his face about, and blessed all the congregation of Israel: (and all the congregation of Israel stood;)

And Solomon stood before the altar of the Lord in the presence of all the congregation of Israel, and spread forth his hands toward heaven.

And he stood, and blessed all the congregation of Israel with a loud voice, saying,

Blessed be the LORD, that hath given rest unto his people Israel, according to all that he promised: there hath not failed one word of all his good promise, which he promised by the hand of Moses his servant.

The LORD our God be with us, as he was with our fathers: let him not leave us, nor forsake us:

I Kings 8:14, 22, 55-57

And he stood before the altar of the Lord in the presence of all the congregation of Israel, and spread forth his hands:

For Solomon had made a brasen scaffold, of five cubits long, and five cubits broad, and three cubits high, and had set it in the midst of the court: and upon it he stood, and kneeled down upon his knees before all the congregation of Israel, and spread forth his hands toward heaven,

And said, O LORD God of Israel, there is no God like thee in the heaven, nor in the earth; which keepest covenant, and shewest mercy unto thy servants, that walk before thee with all their hearts:

II Chronicles 6:12-14

And all the people saw the cloudy pillar stand at the tabernacle door: and all the people rose up and worshipped, every man in his tent door.

Exodus 33:10

After this manner therefore pray ye: Our Father which art in heaven, Hallowed be thy name.

Thy kingdom come. Thy will be done in earth, as it is in heaven.

Give us this day our daily bread.

And forgive us our debts, as we forgive our debtors.

And lead us not into temptation, but deliver us from evil: For thine is the kingdom, and the power, and the glory, for ever. Amen.

For if ye forgive men their trespasses, your heavenly Father will also forgive you:

But if you forgive not men their trespasses, neither will your Father forgive your trespasses.

Matthew 6:5-15

Agreement in Prayer

And God said, Sarah thy wife shall bear thee a son indeed; and thou shalt call his name Isaac: and I will establish my covenant with him for an everlasting covenant, and with his seed after him.

Genesis 17:19

And thou saidst, I will surely do thee good, and make thy seed as the sand of the sea, which cannot be numbered for multitude.

Genesis 32:12

Remember Abraham, Isaac, and Israel, thy servants, to whom thou swarest by thine own self, and saidst unto them, I will multiply your seed as the stars of heaven, and all this land that I have spoken of will I give unto your seed, and they shall inherit it for ever.

Exodus 32:13

And he said, Hearken ye, all Judah, and ye inhabitants of Jerusalem, and thou king Jehoshaphat, Thus saith the Lord unto you, Be not afraid nor dismayed by reason of this great multitude; for the battle is not yours, but God's.

Tomorrow go ye down against them: behold, they come up by the cliff of Ziz; and ye shall find them at the end of the brook, before the wilderness of Jeruel.

Ye shall not need to fight in this battle: set yourselves, stand ye still, and see the salvation of the Lord with you, O Judah and Jerusalem: fear not, nor be dismayed; tomorrow go out against them: for the Lord will be with you.

II Chronicles 20:15-17

My covenant will I not break, nor alter after the thing that is gone out of my lips.

Psalm 89:34

When the Lord shall build up Zion, he shall appear in his glory.

He will regard the prayer of the destitute, and not despise their prayer.

Psalm 102:16, 17

Incline your ear, and come unto me: hear, and your soul shall live; and I will make an everlasting covenant with you, even the sure mercies of David.

Isaiah 55:3

For I the Lord love judgment, I hate robbery for burnt offering; and I will direct their work in truth, and I will make an everlasting covenant with them.

Isaiah 61:8

Behold, the days come, saith the Lord, that I will make a new covenant with the house of Israel, and with the house of Judah:

Not according to the covenant that I made with their fathers in the day that I took them by the hand to bring them out of the land of Egypt; which my covenant they brake, although I was an husband unto them, saith the Lord:

But this shall be the covenant that I will make with the house of Israel; After those days, saith the Lord, I will put my law in their inward parts, and write it in their hearts; and will be their God, and they shall be my people.

And they shall teach no more every man his neighbor, and every man his brother, saying, Know the Lord: for they shall all know me, from the least of them unto the greatest of them, saith the Lord: for I will forgive their iniquity, and I will remember their sin no more.

Jeremiah 31:31-34

O my God, incline thine ear, and hear; open thine eyes, and behold our desolations, and the city which is called by thy name: for we do not present our supplications before thee for our righteousnessess, but for thy great mercies.

O Lord, hear; O Lord, forgive; O Lord, hearken and do; defer not, for thine own sake, O my God: for thy city and thy people are called by thy name.

Daniel 9:18, 19

Again I say unto you, That if two of you shall agree on earth as touching any thing that they shall ask, it shall be done for them of my Father which is in heaven.   *Matthew 18:19*

Christ hath redeemed us from the curse of the law, being made a curse for us: for it is written, Cursed is every one that hangeth on a tree:

That the blessing of Abraham might come on the Gentiles through Jesus Christ; that we might receive the promise of the Spirit through faith.

Brethren, I speak after the manner of men; Though it be but a man's covenant, yet if it be confirmed, no man disannulleth, or addeth thereto.

Now to Abraham and his seed were the promises made. He saith not, And to seeds, as of many; but as of one, And to thy seed, which is Christ.

And this I say, that the covenant, that was confirmed before of God in Christ, the law, which was four hundred and thirty years after, cannot disannul, that it should make the promise of none effect.

For if the inheritance be of the law, it is no more of promise: but God gave it to Abraham by promise.

Wherefore then serveth the law? It was added because of transgressions, till the seed should come to whom the promise was made; and it was ordained by angels in the hand of a mediator.

Now a mediator is not a mediator of one, but God is one.

Is the law then against the promises of God? God forbid: for if there had been a law given which could have given life, verily righteousness should have been by the law.

But the scripture hath concluded all under sin, that the promise by faith of Jesus Christ might be given to them that believe.

But before faith came, we were kept under the law, shut up unto the faith which should afterwards be revealed.

Wherefore the law was our schoolmaster to bring us unto Christ, that we might be justified by faith.

But after that faith is come, we are no longer under a schoolmaster.

For ye are all the children of God by faith in Christ Jesus.

For as many of you as have been baptized into Christ have put on Christ.

There is neither Jew nor Greek, there is neither bond nor free, there is neither male nor female: for ye all are one in Christ Jesus.

And if ye be Christ's, then are ye Abraham's seed, and heirs according to the promise.

Galatians 3:13-29

But now hath he obtained a more excellent ministry, by how much also he is the mediator of a better covenant, which was established upon better promises.

For this is the covenant that I will make with the house of Israel after those days, saith the Lord:

I will put my laws into their minds, and write them in their hearts: and I will be to them a God, and they shall be to me a people:

Hebrews 8:6, 10

To the general assembly and church of the firstborn, which are written in heaven, and to God the Judge of all, and to the spirits of just men made perfect,

And to Jesus the mediator of the new covenant, and to the blood of sprinkling, that speaketh better things than that of Abel.

See that ye refuse not him that speaketh. For if they escaped not who refused him that spake on earth, much more shall not we escape, if we turn away from him that speaketh from heaven:

Hebrews 12:23-25

Now the God of peace, that brought again from the dead our Lord Jesus, that great shepherd of the sheep, through the blood of the everlasting covenant,

Make you perfect in every good work to do his will, working in you that which is well-pleasing in his sight, through Jesus Christ; to whom be glory for ever and ever. Amen.

Hebrews 13:20-21

And he said, I am Abraham's servant.

And the Lord hath blessed my master greatly; and he is become great: and hath given him flocks, and herds, and silver, and gold, and menservants, and maidservants, and camels, and asses.

And Sarah my master's wife bare a son to my master when she was old: and unto him hath he given all that he hath.

And my master made me swear, saying, Thou shalt not take a wife to my son of the daughters of the Canaanites, in whose land I dwell.

But thou shalt go unto my father's house, and to my kindred, and take a wife unto my son.

And I said unto my master, Peradventure the woman will not follow me.

And he said unto me, The Lord, before whom I walk, will send his angel with thee, and prosper thy way; and thou shalt take a wife for my son of my kindred, and of my father's house:

Genesis 24:34-40

And he shall turn the heart of the fathers to the children, and the heart of the children to their fathers, lest I come and smite the earth with a curse.

Malachi 4:6

And the whole multitude of the people were praying without at the time of incense.

Luke 1:10

And there came a fear on all: and they glorified God, saying, That a great prophet is risen up among us; and, That God hath visited his people.

Luke 7:16

-248-

And when they heard that, they lifted up their voice to God with one accord, and said, Lord, thou art God, which hast made heaven, and earth, and the sea, and all that in them is:

Acts 4:24

And when he had considered the thing, he came to the house of Mary the mother of John, whose surname was Mark; where many were gathered together praying.

Acts 12:12

So Abraham prayed unto God: and God healed Abimelech, and his wife, and his maidservants; and they bare children.

For the Lord had fast closed up all the wombs of the house of Abimelech, because of Sarah Abraham's wife.

Genesis 20:17, 18

And Isaac entreated the Lord for his wife, because she was barren: and the Lord was entreated of him, and Rebekah his wife conceived.

Genesis 25:21

Then the woman came and told her husband, saying, A man of God came unto me, and his countenance was like the countenance of an angel of God, very terrible: but I asked him not whence he was, neither told he me his name:

But he said unto me, Behold, thou shalt conceive, and bear a son; and now drink no wine nor strong drink, neither eat any unclean thing: for the child shall be a Nazarite to God from the womb to the day of his death.

Then Manoah entreated the LORD, and said, O my Lord, let the man of God which thou didst send come again unto us, and teach us what we shall do unto the child that shall be born.

And the angel of the LORD said unto Manoah, Of all that I said unto the woman let her beware.

And the woman bare a son, and called his name Samson: and the child grew, and the LORD blessed him.

Judges 13:6-8, 13, 24

And when we had accomplished those days, we departed and went our way; and they all brought us on our way, with wives and children, till we were out of the city: and we kneeled down on the shore and prayed.

Acts 21:5

A devout man, and one that feared God with all his house, which gave much alms to the people, and prayed to God alway.

And Cornelius said, Four days ago I was fasting until this hour; and at the ninth hour I prayed in my house, and, behold, a man stood before me in bright clothing,

And said, Cornelius, thy prayer is heard, and thine alms are had in remembrance in the sight of God.

Acts 10:2, 30-31

And she was in bitterness of soul, and prayed unto the LORD, and wept sore.

And she vowed a vow, and said, O LORD of hosts, if thou wilt indeed look on the affliction of thine handmaid, and remember me, and not forget thine handmaid, but wilt give unto thine handmaid a man child, then I will give him unto the LORD all the days of his life, and there shall no razor come upon his head.

And it came to pass, as she continued praying before the LORD, that Eli marked her mouth.

Now Hannah, she spake in her heart; only her lips moved, but her voice was not heard: therefore Eli thought she had been drunken.

And Eli said unto her, How long wilt thou be drunken? put away thy wine from thee.

And Hannah answered and said, No, my lord, I am a woman of a sorrowful spirit: I have drunk neither wine nor strong drink, but have poured out my soul before the LORD.

Count not thine handmaid for a daughter of Belial: for out of the abundance of my complaint and grief have I spoken hitherto.

Then Eli answered and said, Go in peace: and the God of Israel grant thee thy petition that thou hast asked of him.

And she said, Let thine handmaid find grace in thy sight. So the woman went her way, and did eat, and her countenance was no more sad.

And they rose up in the morning early, and worshipped before the Lord, and returned, and came to their house to Ramah: and Elkanah knew his wife; and the Lord remembered her.

Wherefore it came to pass, when the time was come about after Hannah had conceived, that she bare a son, and called his name Samuel, saying, Because I have asked him of the LORD.

And she said, Oh my lord, as thy soul liveth, my lord, I am the woman that stood by thee here, praying unto the LORD.

For this child I prayed; and the LORD hath given me my petition which I asked of him:

Therefore also I have lent him to the LORD: as long as he liveth he shall be lent to the LORD. And he worshipped the LORD there.

I Samuel 1:10-20, 26-28

But the angel said unto him, Fear not, Zacharias: for thy prayer is heard; and thy wife Elisabeth shall bear thee a son, and thou shalt call his name John.

Luke 1:13

Blessed is the nation whose God is the Lord; and the people whom he hath chosen for his own inheritance.

Psalm 33:12

As I besought thee to abide still at Ephesus, when I went into Macedonia, that thou mightest charge some that they teach no other doctrine,

But we know that the law is good, if a man use it lawfully;

I Timothy 1:3, 8

I exhort therefore that, first of all, supplications, prayers, intercessions, and giving of thanks, be made for all men;

For kings, and for all that are in authority; that we may lead a quiet and peaceable life in all godliness and honesty.

For this is good and acceptable in the sight of God our Saviour;

I Timothy 2:1-3

Praying the Psalms

God's Provision

PSALM 1

Blessed is the man that walketh not in the counsel of the ungodly, nor standeth in the way of sinners, nor sitteth in the seat of the scornful.

But his delight is in the law of the Lord; and in his law doth he meditate day and night.

And he shall be like a tree planted by the rivers of water, that bringeth forth his fruit in his season; his leaf also shall not wither; and whatsoever he doeth shall prosper.

The ungodly are not so: but are like the chaff which the wind driveth away.

Therefore the ungodly shall not stand in the judgment, nor sinners in the congregation of the righteous.

For the LORD knoweth the way of the righteous: but the way of the ungodly shall perish.

God's Protection

PSALM 5

Give ear to my words, O LORD; consider my meditation.

Hearken unto the voice of my cry, my King, and my God: for unto thee will I pray.

My voice shalt thou hear in the morning, O LORD; in the morning will I direct my prayer unto thee, and will look up.

For thou art not a God that hath pleasure in wickedness: neither shall evil dwell with thee.

The foolish shall not stand in thy sight: thou hatest all workers of iniquity.

Thou shalt destroy them that speak leasing: the LORD will abhor the bloody and deceitful man.

But as for me, I will come into thy house in the multitude of thy mercy: and in thy fear will I worship toward thy holy temple.

Lead me, O LORD. in thy righteousness because of mine enemies; make thy way straight before my face.

For there is no faithfulness in their mouth; their inward part is very wickedness; their throat is an open sepulchre; they flatter with their tongue.

Destroy thou them, O God; let them fall by their own counsels; cast them out in the multitude of their transgressions; for they have rebelled against thee.

But let all those that put their trust in thee rejoice: let them ever shout for joy, because thou defendest them: let them also that love thy name be joyful in thee.

For thou, LORD, wilt bless the righteous; with favor wilt thou compass him as with a shield.

Praise to the Lord

PSALM 8

O LORD our Lord, how excellent is thy name in all the earth! who hast set thy glory above the heavens.

Out of the mouth of babes and sucklings hast thou ordained strength because of thine enemies, that thou mightest still the enemy and the avenger.

When I consider thy heavens, the work of thy fingers, the moon and the stars, which thou hast ordained;

What is man, that thou art mindful of him? and the son of man, that thou visitest him?

For thou hast made him a little lower than the angels, and hast crowned him with glory and honor.

Thou madest him to have dominion over the works of thy hands; thou hast put all things under his feet:

All sheep and oxen, yea, and the beasts of the field;

The fowl of the air, and the fish of the sea, and whatsoever passeth through the paths of the seas.

O LORD our Lord, how excellent is thy name in all the earth!

Our Preservation

PSALM 16

Preserve me, O God: for in thee do I put my trust.

O my soul, thou hast said unto the LORD, Thou art my Lord: my goodness extendeth not to thee;

But to the saints that are in the earth, and to the excellent, in whom is all my delight.

Their sorrows shall be multiplied that hasten after another god: their drink offerings of blood will I not offer, nor take up their names into my lips.

The LORD is the portion of mine inheritance and of my cup: thou maintainest my lot.

The lines are fallen unto me in pleasant places; yea, I have a goodly heritage.

I will bless the LORD, who hath given me counsel: my reins also instruct me in the night seasons.

I have set the LORD always before me: because he is at my right hand, I shall not be moved.

Therefore my heart is glad, and my glory rejoiceth: my flesh also shall rest in hope.

For thou wilt not leave my soul in hell; neither wilt thou suffer thine Holy One to see corruption.

Thou wilt show me the path of life: in thy presence is fulness of joy; at thy right hand there are pleasures for evermore.

Our Comfort

PSALM 23

The Lord is my shepherd; I shall not want.

He maketh me to lie down in green pastures; he leadeth me beside the still waters.

He restoreth my soul: he leadeth me in the paths of righteousness for his name's sake.

Yea, though I walk through the valley of the shadow of death, I will fear no evil: for thou art with me; thy rod and thy staff they comfort me.

Thou preparest a table before me in the presence of mine enemies: thou anointest my head with oil; my cup runneth over.

Surely goodness and mercy shall follow me all the days of my life: and I will dwell in the house of the LORD for ever.

God's Sovereignty
PSALM 24

The earth is the LORD's, and the fulness thereof; the world, and they that dwell therein.

For he hath founded it upon the seas, and established it upon the floods.

Who shall ascend into the hill of the LORD? Or who shall stand in his holy place?

He that hath clean hands, and a pure heart; who hath not lifted up his soul unto vanity, nor sworn deceitfully.

He shall receive the blessing from the LORD, and righteousness from the God of his salvation.

This is the generation of them that seek him, that seek thy face, O Jacob. Selah.

Lift up your heads, O ye gates; and be ye lifted up, ye everlasting doors; and the King of glory shall come in.

Who is this King of glory? The LORD strong and mighty, the LORD mighty in battle.

Lift up your heads, O ye gates; even lift them up, ye everlasting doors; and the King of glory shall come in.

Who is this King of glory? The LORD of hosts, he is the King of glory. Selah.

God's Strength

PSALM 27

The LORD is my light and my salvation; whom shall I fear? The LORD is the strength of my life; of whom shall I be afraid?

When the wicked, even mine enemies and my foes, came upon me to eat up my flesh, they stumbled and fell.

Though a host should encamp against me, my heart shall not fear: though war should rise against me, in this will I be confident.

One thing have I desired of the LORD, that will I seek after; that I may dwell in the house of the LORD all the days of my life, to behold the beauty of the LORD, and to inquire in his temple.

For in the time of trouble he shall hide me in his pavilion: in the secret of his tabernacle shall he hide me; he shall set me up upon a rock.

And now shall mine head be lifted up above mine enemies round about me: therefore will I offer in his tabernacle sacrifices of joy; I will sing, yea, I will sing praises unto the LORD.

Hear, O LORD, when I cry with my voice: have mercy also upon me, and answer me.

When thou saidst, Seek ye my face; my heart said unto thee, Thy face, LORD, will I seek.

Hide not thy face far from me; put not thy servant away in anger: thou hast been my help;

leave me not, neither forsake me, O God of my salvation.

When my father and my mother forsake me, then the LORD will take me up.

Teach me thy way, O LORD, and lead me in a plain path, because of mine enemies.

Deliver me not over unto the will of mine enemies: for false witnesses are risen up against me, and such as breathe out cruelty.

I had fainted, unless I had believed to see the goodness of the LORD in the land of the living.

Wait on the LORD: be of good courage, and he shall strengthen thine heart: wait, I say, on the LORD.

Our Protection

PSALM 35

Plead my cause, O LORD, with them that strive with me: fight against them that fight against me.

Take hold of shield and buckler, and stand up for mine help.

Draw out also the spear, and stop the way against them that persecute me: say unto my soul, I am thy salvation.

Let them be confounded and put to shame that seek after my soul: let them be turned back and brought to confusion that devise my hurt.

Let them be as chaff before the wind: and let the angel of the LORD chase them.

Let their way be dark and slippery: and let the angel of the LORD persecute them.

For without cause have they hid for me their net in a pit, which without cause they have digged for my soul.

Let destruction come upon him at unawares; and let his net that he hath hid catch himself: into that very destruction let him fall.

And my soul shall be joyful in the LORD: it shall rejoice in his salvation.

All my bones shall say, LORD, who is like unto thee, which deliverest the poor from him that is too strong for him, yea, the poor and the needy from him that spoileth him?

False witnesses did rise up; they laid to my charge things that I knew not.

They rewarded me evil for good to the spoiling of my soul.

But as for me, when they were sick, my clothing was sackcloth: I humbled my soul with fasting; and my prayer returned into mine own bosom.

I behaved myself as though he had been my friend or brother: I bowed down heavily, as one that mourneth for his mother.

But in mine adversity they rejoiced, and gathered themselves together: yea, the abjects gathered themselves together against me, and I knew it not; they did tear me, and ceased not:

With hypocritical mockers in feasts, they gnashed upon me with their teeth.

Lord, how long wilt thou look on? Rescue my soul from their destructions, my darling from the lions.

I will give thee thanks in the great congregation: I will praise thee among much people.

Let not them that are mine enemies wrongfully rejoice over me: neither let them wink with the eye that hate me without a cause.

For they speak not peace: but they devise deceitful matters against them that are quiet in the land.

Yea, they opened their mouth wide against me, and said, Aha, aha, our eye hath seen it.

This thou hast seen, O LORD: keep not

silence: O Lord, be not far from me.

Stir up thyself, and awake to my judgment, even unto my cause, my God and my Lord.

Judge me, O LORD my God, according to thy righteousness; and let them not rejoice over me.

Let them not say in their hearts, Ah, so would we have it: let them not say, We have swallowed him up.

Let them be ashamed and brought to confusion together that rejoice at mine hurt: let them be clothed with shame and dishonor that magnify themselves against me.

Let them shout for joy, and be glad, that favor my righteous cause: yea, let them say continually, Let the LORD be magnified, which hath pleasure in the prosperity of his servant.

And my tongue shall speak of thy righteousness and of thy praise all the day long.

God's Compassion

PSALM 41

Blessed is he that considereth the poor: the Lord will deliver him in time of trouble.

The Lord will preserve him, and keep him alive; and he shall be blessed upon the earth: and thou wilt not deliver him unto the will of his enemies.

The Lord will strengthen him upon the bed of languishing: thou wilt make all his bed in his sickness.

I said, LORD, be merciful unto me: heal my soul; for I have sinned against thee.

Mine enemies speak evil of me, When shall he die, and his name perish?

And if he come to see me, he speaketh vanity: his heart gathereth iniquity to itself; when he goeth abroad, he telleth it.

All that hate me whisper together against me: against me do they devise my hurt.

An evil disease, say they, cleaveth fast unto him: and now that he lieth he shall rise up no more.

Yea, mine own familiar friend, in whom I trusted, which did eat of my bread, hath lifted up his heel against me.

But thou, O LORD, be merciful unto me, and raise me up, that I may requite them.

By this I know that thou favorest me, because mine enemy doth not triumph over me.

And as for me, thou upholdest me in mine integrity, and settest me before thy face for ever.

Blessed be the LORD God of Israel from everlasting, and to everlasting. Amen, and Amen.

Our Yearning for the Lord

PSALM 42

As the hart panteth after the water brooks, so panteth my soul after thee, O God.

My soul thirsteth for God, for the living God: when shall I come and appear before God?

My tears have been my meat day and night, while they continually say unto me, Where is thy God?

When I remember these things, I pour out my soul in me: for I had gone with the multitude, I went with them to the house of God, with the voice of joy and praise, with a multitude that kept holyday.

Why art thou cast down, O my soul? And why art thou disquieted in me? Hope thou in God: for I shall yet praise him for the help of his countenance.

O my God, my soul is cast down within me: therefore will I remember thee from the land of Jordan, and of the Hermonites, from the hill Mizar.

Deep calleth unto deep at the noise of thy waterspouts: all thy waves and thy billows are gone over me.

Yet the LORD will command his lovingkindness in the daytime, and in the night his song shall be with me, and my prayer unto the God of my life.

I will say unto God my rock, why hast thou forgotten me? Why go I mourning because of the oppression of the enemy?

As with a sword in my bones, mine enemies reproach me; while they say daily unto me, Where is thy God?

Why art thou cast down, O my soul? And why art thou disquieted within me? Hope thou in God: for I shall yet praise him, who is the health of my countenance, and my God.

God's Power, Presence, and Peace

PSALM 46

God is our refuge and strength, a very present help in trouble.

Therefore will not we fear, though the earth be removed, and though the mountains be carried into the midst of the sea;

Though the waters thereof roar and be troubled, though the mountains shake with the swelling thereof. Selah.

There is a river, the streams whereof shall make glad the city of God, the holy place of the tabernacles of the Most High.

God is in the midst of her; she shall not be moved: God shall help her, and that right early.

The heathen raged, the kingdoms were moved: he uttered his voice, the earth melted.

The LORD of hosts is with us; the God of Jacob is our refuge. Selah.

Come, behold the works of the LORD, what desolations he hath made in the earth.

He maketh wars to cease unto the end of the earth; he breaketh the bow, and cutteth the spear in sunder; he burneth the chariot in the fire.

Be still, and know that I am God: I will be exalted among the heathen, I will be exalted in the earth.

The LORD of hosts is with us; the God of Jacob is our refuge. Selah.

God's Forgiveness

PSALM 51

Have mercy upon me, O God, according to thy lovingkindness: according unto the multitude of thy tender mercies blot out my transgressions.

Wash me thoroughly from mine iniquity, and cleanse me from my sin.

For I acknowledge my transgressions: and my sin is ever before me.

Against thee, thee only, have I sinned, and done this evil in thy sight: that thou mightest be justified when thou speakest, and be clear when thou judgest.

Behold, I was shapen in iniquity; and in sin did my mother conceive me.

Behold, thou desirest truth in the inward parts: and in the hidden part thou shalt make me to know wisdom.

Purge me with hyssop, and I shall be clean: wash me, and I shall be whiter than snow.

Make me to hear joy and gladness; that the bones which thou hast broken may rejoice.

Hide thy face from my sins, and blot out all mine iniquities.

Create in me a clean heart, O God; and renew a right spirit within me.

Cast me not away from thy presence: and take not thy Holy Spirit from me.

Restore unto me the joy of thy salvation: and uphold me with thy free Spirit.

Then will I teach transgressors thy ways; and sinners shall be converted unto thee.

Deliver me from bloodguiltiness, O God, thou God of my salvation: and my tongue shall sing aloud of thy righteousness.

O Lord, open thou my lips; and my mouth shall show forth thy praise.

For thou desirest not sacrifice; else would I give it: thou delightest not in burnt offering.

The sacrifices of God are a broken spirit: a broken and a contrite heart, O God, thou wilt not despise.

Do good in thy good pleasure unto Zion: build thou the walls of Jerusalem.

Then shalt thou be pleased with the sacrifices of righteousness, with burnt offering and whole burnt offering: then shall they offer bullocks upon thine altar.

Our Petitions

PSALM 90

LORD, thou hast been our dwelling place in all generations.

Before the mountains were brought forth, or ever thou hadst formed the earth and the world, even from everlasting to everlasting, thou art God.

Thou turnest man to destruction; and sayest, Return, ye children of men.

For a thousand years in thy sight are but as yesterday when it is past, and as a watch in the night.

Thou carriest them away as with a flood; they are as a sleep: in the morning they are like grass which groweth up.

In the morning it flourisheth, and groweth up; in the evening it is cut down, and withereth.

For we are consumed by thine anger, and by thy wrath are we troubled.

Thou hast set our iniquities before thee, our secret sins in the light of thy countenance.

For all our days are passed away in thy wrath: we spend our years as a tale that is told.

The days of our years are threescore years and ten; and if by reason of strength they be fourscore years, yet is their strength labor and sorrow; for it is soon cut off, and we fly away.

Who knoweth the power of thine anger? Even according to thy fear, so is thy wrath.

So teach us to number our days, that we may apply our hearts unto wisdom.

Return, O LORD, how long? And let it repent thee concerning thy servants.

O satisfy us early with thy mercy; that we may rejoice and be glad all our days.

Make us glad according to the days wherein thou hast afflicted us, and the years wherein we have seen evil.

Let thy work appear unto thy servants, and thy glory unto their children.

And let the beauty of the LORD our God be upon us: and establish thou the work of our hands upon us; yea, the work of our hands establish thou it.

God's Greatness

PSALM 102

Hear my prayer, O LORD, and let my cry come unto thee.

Hide not thy face from me in the day when I am in trouble; incline thine ear unto me: in the day when I call answer me speedily.

For my days are consumed like smoke, and my bones are burned as a hearth.

My heart is smitten, and withered like grass; so that I forget to eat my bread.

By reason of the voice of my groaning my bones cleave to my skin.

I am like a pelican of the wilderness: I am like an owl of the desert.

I watch, and am as a sparrow alone upon the housetop.

Mine enemies reproach me all the day; and they that are mad against me are sworn against me.

For I have eaten ashes like bread, and mingled my drink with weeping,

Because of thine indignation and thy wrath: for thou hast lifted me up, and cast me down.

My days are like a shadow that declineth; and I am withered like grass.

But thou, O LORD, shalt endure for ever; and thy remembrance unto all generations.

Thou shalt arise, and have mercy upon Zion: for the time to favor her, yea, the set time, is come.

For thy servants take pleasure in her stones, and favor the dust thereof.

So the heathen shall fear the name of the LORD, and all the kings of the earth thy glory.

When the LORD shall build up Zion, he shall appear in his glory.

He will regard the prayer of the destitute, and not despise their prayer.

This shall be written for the generation to come: and the people which shall be created shall praise the LORD.

For he hath looked down from the height of his sanctuary; from heaven did the LORD behold the earth;

To hear the groaning of the prisoner; to loose those that are appointed to death;

To declare the name of the LORD in Zion, and his praise in Jerusalem;

When the people are gathered together, and the kingdoms, to serve the LORD.

He weakened my strength in the way; he shortened my days.

I said, O my God, take me not away in the midst of my days: thy years are throughout all generations.

Of old hast thou laid the foundation of the earth: and the heavens are the work of thy hands.

They shall perish, but thou shalt endure: yea, all of them shall wax old like a garment; as a vesture shalt thou change them, and they shall have no end.

The children of thy servants shall continue, and their seed shall be established before thee.

PSALM 103

Bless the LORD, O my soul: and all that is within me, bless his holy name.

Bless the LORD, O my soul, and forget not all his benefits:

Who forgiveth all thine iniquities; who healeth all thy diseases;

Who redeemeth thy life from destruction; who crowneth thee with lovingkindness and tender mercies;

Who satisfieth thy mouth with good things; so that thy youth is renewed like the eagle's.

The LORD executeth righteousness and judgment for all that are oppressed.

He made known his ways unto Moses, his acts unto the children of Israel.

The LORD is merciful and gracious, slow to anger, and plenteous in mercy.

He will not always chide: neither will he keep his anger for ever.

He hath not dealt with us after our sins; nor rewarded us according to our iniquities.

For as the heaven is high above the earth, so great is his mercy toward them that fear him.

As far as the east is from the west, so far hath he removed our transgressions from us.

Like as a father pitieth his children, so the LORD pitieth them that fear him.

For he knoweth our frame; he remembereth that we are dust.

As for man, his days are as grass: as a flower of the field, so he flourisheth.

For the wind passeth over it, and it is gone; and the place thereof shall know it no more.

But the mercy of the LORD is from everlasting to everlasting upon them that fear him, and his righteousness unto children's children;

To such as keep his covenant, and to those that remember his commandments to do them.

The LORD hath prepared his throne in the heavens; and his kingdom ruleth over all.

Bless the LORD, ye his angels, that excel in strength, that do his commandments, hearkening unto the voice of his word.

Bless ye the LORD, all ye his hosts; ye ministers of his, that do his pleasure.

Bless the LORD, all his works in all places of his dominion: bless the LORD, O my soul.

PSALM 105

O give thanks unto the LORD; call upon his name: make known his deeds among the people.

Sing unto him, sing psalms unto him: talk ye of all his wondrous works.

Glory ye in his holy name: let the heart of them rejoice that seek the LORD.

Seek the LORD, and his strength: seek his face evermore.

Remember his marvelous works that he hath done; his wonders, and the judgments of his mouth;

O ye seed of Abraham his servant, ye children of Jacob his chosen.

He is the LORD our God: his judgments are in all the earth.

He hath remembered his covenant for ever, the word which he commanded to a thousand generations.

Which covenant he made with Abraham, and his oath unto Isaac;

And confirmed the same unto Jacob for a law, and to Israel for an everlasting covenant:

Saying, Unto thee will I give the land of Canaan, the lot of your inheritance.

When they were but a few men in number; yea, very few, and strangers in it;

When they went from one nation to another, from one kingdom to another people;

He suffered no man to do them wrong: yea, he reproved kings for their sakes;

Saying, Touch not mine anointed, and do my prophets no harm.

Moreover he called for a famine upon the land: he brake the whole staff of bread.

He sent a man before them, even Joseph, who was sold for a servant:

Whose feet they hurt with fetters: he was laid in iron:

Until the time that his word came: the word of the LORD tried him.

The king sent and loosed him; even the ruler of the people, and let him go free.

He made him lord of his house, and ruler of all his substance:

To bind his princes at his pleasure; and teach his senators wisdom.

Israel also came into Egypt; and Jacob sojourned in the land of Ham.

And he increased his people greatly; and made them stronger than their enemies.

He turned their heart to hate his people, to deal subtilely with his servants.

He sent Moses his servant; and Aaron whom he had chosen.

They showed his signs among them, and wonders in the land of Ham.

He sent darkness, and made it dark; and they rebelled not against his word.

He turned their waters into blood, and slew their fish.

Their land brought forth frogs in abundance, in the chambers of their kings.

He spake, and there came divers sorts of flies, and lice in all their coasts.

He gave them hail for rain, and flaming fire in their land.

He smote their vines also and their fig trees; and brake the trees of their coasts.

He spake, and the locusts came, and caterpillars, and that without number,

And did eat up all the herbs in their land, and devoured the fruit of their ground.

He smote also all the firstborn in their land, the chief of all their strength.

He brought them forth also with silver and gold: and there was not one feeble person among their tribes.

Egypt was glad when they departed: for the fear of them fell upon them.

He spread a cloud for a covering; and fire to give light in the night.

The people asked, and he brought quails, and satisfied them with the bread of heaven.

He opened the rock, and the waters gushed out; they ran in the dry places like a river.

For he remembered his holy promise, and Abraham his servant.

And he brought forth his people with joy, and his chosen with gladness:

And gave them the lands of the heathen: and they inherited the labor of the people;

That they might observe his statutes, and keep his laws. Praise ye the LORD.

God's Mercy

PSALM 107

O give thanks unto the LORD, for he is good: for his mercy endureth for ever.

Let the redeemed of the LORD say so, whom he hath redeemed from the hand of the enemy;

And gathered them out of the lands, from the east, and from the west, from the north, and from the south.

They wandered in the wilderness in a solitary way; they found no city to dwell in.

Hungry and thirsty, their soul fainted in them.

Then they cried unto the LORD in their trouble, and he delivered them out of their distresses.

And he led them forth by the right way, that they might go to a city of habitation.

Oh that men would praise the LORD for his goodness, and for his wonderful works to the children of men!

For he satisfieth the longing soul, and filleth the hungry soul with goodness.

Such as sit in darkness and in the shadow of death, being bound in affliction and iron;

Because they rebelled against the words of God, and condemned the counsel of the Most High:

Therefore he brought down their heart with labor; they fell down, and there was none to help.

Then they cried unto the LORD in their trouble, and he saved them out of their distresses.

He brought them out of darkness and the shadow of death, and brake their bands in sunder.

Oh that men would praise the LORD for his goodness, and for his wonderful works to the children of men!

For he hath broken the gates of brass, and cut the bars of iron in sunder.

Fools, because of their transgression, and because of their iniquities, are afflicted.

Their soul abhorreth all manner of meat; and they draw near unto the gates of death.

Then they cry unto the LORD in their trouble, and he saveth them out of their distresses.

He sent his word, and healed them, and delivered them from their destructions.

Oh that men would praise the LORD for his goodness, and for his wonderful works to the children of men!

And let them sacrifice the sacrifices of thanksgiving, and declare his works with rejoicing.

They that go down to the sea in ships, that do business in great waters;

These see the works of the LORD, and his wonders in the deep.

For he commandeth, and raiseth the stormy wind, which lifteth up the waves thereof.

They mount up to the heaven, they go down again to the depths: their soul is melted because of trouble.

They reel to and fro, and stagger like a drunken man, and are at their wit's end.

Then they cry unto the LORD in their trouble, and he bringeth them out of their distresses.

He maketh the storm a calm, so that the waves thereof are still.

Then are they glad because they be quiet; so he bringeth them unto their desired haven.

Oh that men would praise the LORD for his goodness, and for his wonderful works to the children of men!

Let them exalt him also in the congregation of the people, and praise him in the assembly of the elders.

He turneth rivers into a wilderness, and the watersprings into dry ground;

A fruitful land into barrenness, for the wickedness of them that dwell therein.

He turneth the wilderness into a standing water, and dry ground into watersprings.

And there he maketh the hungry to dwell, that they may prepare a city for habitation;

And sow the fields, and plant vineyards, which may yield fruits of increase.

He blesseth them also, so that they are multiplied greatly; and suffereth not their cattle to decrease.

Again, they are minished and brought low through oppression, affliction, and sorrow.

He poureth contempt upon princes, and

causeth them to wander in the wilderness, where there is no way.

Yet setteth he the poor on high from affliction, and maketh him families like a flock.

The righteous shall see it, and rejoice: and all iniquity shall stop her mouth.

Whoso is wise, and will observe these things, even they shall understand the lovingkindness of the LORD.

God's Purity

PSALM 19

The heavens declare the glory of God; and the firmament showeth his handiwork.

Day unto day uttereth speech, and night unto night showeth knowledge.

There is no speech nor language, where their voice is not heard.

Their line is gone out through all the earth, and their words to the end of the world. In them hath he set a tabernacle for the sun,

Which is as a bridegroom coming out of his chamber, and rejoiceth as a strong man to run a race.

His going forth is from the end of the heaven, and his circuit unto the ends of it: and there is nothing hid from the heat thereof.

The law of the LORD is perfect, converting the soul: the testimony of the LORD is sure, making wise the simple.

The statutes of the LORD are right, rejoicing the heart: the commandment of the LORD is pure, enlightening the eyes.

The fear of the LORD is clean, enduring for ever: the judgments of the LORD are true and righteous altogether.

More to be desired are they than gold, yea, then much fine gold: sweeter also than honey and the honeycomb.

Moreover by them is thy servant warned: and in keeping of them there is great reward.

Who can understand his errors? Cleanse thou me from secret faults.

Keep back thy servant also from presumptuous sins; let them not have dominion over me: then shall I be upright, and I shall be innocent from the great transgression.

Let the words of my mouth, and the meditation of my heart, be acceptable in thy sight, O LORD, my strength, and my redeemer.

Our Purity

PSALM 119

Blessed are the undefiled in the way, who walk in the law of the LORD.

Blessed are they that keep his testimonies, and that seek him with the whole heart.

They also do no iniquity: they walk in his ways.

Thou hast commanded us to keep thy precepts diligently.

O that my ways were directed to keep thy statutes!

Then shall I not be ashamed, when I have respect unto all thy commandments.

I will praise thee with uprightness of heart, when I shall have learned thy righteous judgments.

I will keep thy statutes: O forsake me not utterly.

Wherewithal shall a young man cleanse his way? By taking heed thereto according to thy word.

With my whole heart have I sought thee: O let me not wander from thy commandments.

Thy word have I hid in mine heart, that I might not sin against thee.

Blessed art thou, O LORD: teach me thy statutes.

With my lips have I declared all the judgments of thy mouth.

I have rejoiced in the way of thy testimonies, as much as in all riches.

I will meditate in thy precepts, and have respect unto thy ways.

I will delight myself in thy statutes: I will not forget thy word.

Deal bountifully with thy servant, that I may live, and keep thy word.

Open thou mine eyes, that I may behold wondrous things out of thy law.

I am a stranger in the earth: hide not thy commandments from me.

My soul breaketh for the longing that it hath unto thy judgments at all times.

Thou hast rebuked the proud that are cursed, which do err from thy commandments.

Remove from me reproach and contempt; for I have kept thy testimonies.

Princes also did sit and speak against me: but thy servant did meditate in thy statutes.

Thy testimonies also are my delight, and my counselors.

My soul cleaveth unto the dust: quicken thou me according to thy word.

I have declared my ways, and thou heardest me: teach me thy statutes.

Make me to understand the way of thy precepts: so shall I talk of thy wondrous works.

My soul melteth for heaviness: strengthen thou me according unto thy word.

Remove from me the way of lying: and grant me thy law graciously.

I have chosen the way of truth: thy judgments have I laid before me.

I have stuck unto thy testimonies: O LORD, put me not to shame.

I will run the way of thy commandments, when thou shalt enlarge my heart.

Teach me, O LORD, the way of thy statutes; and I shall keep it unto the end.

Give me understanding, and I shall keep thy law; yea, I shall observe it with my whole heart.

Make me to go in the path of thy commandments; for therein do I delight.

Incline my heart unto thy testimonies, and not to covetousness.

Turn away mine eyes from beholding vanity; and quicken thou me in thy way.

Stablish thy word unto thy servant, who is devoted to thy fear.

Turn away my reproach which I fear: for thy judgments are good.

Behold, I have longed after thy precepts: quicken me in thy righteousness.

Let thy mercies come also unto me, O LORD, even thy salvation, according to thy word.

So shall I have wherewith to answer him that reproacheth me: for I trust in thy word.

And take not the word of truth utterly out of my mouth; for I have hoped in thy judgments.

So shall I keep thy law continually for ever and ever.

And I will walk at liberty: for I seek thy precepts.

I will speak of thy testimonies also before kings, and will not be ashamed.

And I will delight myself in thy commandments, which I have loved.

My hands also will I lift up unto thy commandments, which I have loved; and I will meditate in thy statutes.

Remember the word unto thy servant, upon which thou hast caused me to hope.

This is my comfort in my affliction: for thy word hath quickened me.

The proud have had me greatly in derision: yet have I not declined from thy law.

I remembered thy judgments of old, O LORD; and have comforted myself.

Horror hath taken hold upon me because of the wicked that forsake thy law.

Thy statutes have been my songs in the house of my pilgrimage.

I have remembered thy name, O LORD, in the night, and have kept thy law.

This I had, because I kept thy precepts.

Thou art my portion, O LORD: I have said that I would keep thy words.

I entreated thy favor with my whole heart: be merciful unto me according to thy word.

I thought on my ways, and turned my feet unto thy testimonies.

I made haste, and delayed not to keep thy commandments.

The bands of the wicked have robbed me: but I have not forgotten thy law.

At midnight I will rise to give thanks unto thee because of thy righteous judgments.

I am a companion of all them that fear thee, and of them that keep thy precepts.

The earth, O LORD, is full of thy mercy: teach me thy statutes.

Thou hast dealt well with thy servant, O LORD, according unto thy word.

Teach me good judgment and knowledge: for I have believed thy commandments.

Before I was afflicted I went astray: but now have I kept thy word.

Thou art good, and doest good: teach me thy statutes.

The proud have forged a lie against me: but I will keep thy precepts with my whole heart.

Their heart is as fat as grease: but I delight in thy law.

It is good for me that I have been afflicted; that I might learn thy statutes.

The law of thy mouth is better unto me than thousands of gold and silver.

Thy hands have made me and fashioned me: give me understanding, that I may learn thy commandments.

They that fear thee will be glad when they see me; because I have hoped in thy word.

I know, O LORD, that thy judgments are right, and that thou in faithfulness hast afflicted me.

Let, I pray thee, thy merciful kindness be for my comfort, according to thy word unto thy servant.

Let thy tender mercies come unto me, that I may live: for thy law is my delight.

Let the proud be ashamed; for they dealt perversely with me without a cause: but I will meditate in thy precepts.

Let those that fear thee turn unto me, and those that have known thy testimonies.

Let my heart be sound in thy statutes; that I be not ashamed.

My soul fainteth for thy salvation: but I hope in thy word.

Mine eyes fail for thy word, saying, When wilt thou comfort me?

For I am become like a bottle in the smoke; yet do I not forget thy statutes.

How many are the days of thy servant? When wilt thou execute judgment on them that persecute me?

The proud have digged pits for me, which are not after thy law.

All thy commandments are faithful: they persecute me wrongfully; help thou me.

They had almost consumed me upon earth; but I forsook not thy precepts.

Quicken me after thy lovingkindness; so shall I keep the testimony of thy mouth.

For ever, O LORD, thy word is settled in heaven.

Thy faithfulness is unto all generations: thou hast established the earth, and it abideth.

They continue this day according to thine ordinances: for all are thy servants.

Unless thy law had been my delights, I should then have perished in mine affliction.

I will never forget thy precepts: for with them thou hast quickened me.

I am thine, save me; for I have sought thy precepts.

The wicked have waited for me to destroy me: but I will consider thy testimonies.

I have seen an end of all perfection: but thy commandment is exceeding broad.

O how love I thy law! It is my meditation all the day.

Thou through thy commandments hast made me wiser than mine enemies: for they are ever with me.

I have more understanding than all my teachers: for thy testimonies are my meditation.

I understand more than the ancients, because I keep thy precepts.

I have refrained my feet from every evil way, that I might keep thy word.

I have not departed from thy judgments: for thou hast taught me.

How sweet are thy words unto my taste! yea, sweeter than honey to my mouth.

Through thy precepts I get understanding: therefore I hate every false way.

Thy word is a lamp unto my feet, and a light unto my path.

I have sworn, and I will perform it, that I will keep thy righteous judgments.

I am afflicted very much: quicken me, O LORD, according unto thy word.

Accept, I beseech thee, the freewill offering of my mouth, O LORD, and teach me thy judgments.

My soul is continually in my hand: yet do I not forget thy law.

The wicked have laid a snare for me: yet I erred not from thy precepts.

Thy testimonies have I taken as a heritage for ever: for they are the rejoicing of my heart.

I have inclined mine heart to perform thy statutes always, even unto the end.

I hate vain thoughts: but thy law do I love.

Thou art my hiding place and my shield: I hope in thy word.

Depart from me, ye evildoers: for I will keep the commandments of my God.

Uphold me according unto thy word, that I may live: and let me not be ashamed of my hope.

Hold thou me up, and I shall be safe: and I will have respect unto thy statutes continually.

Thou hast trodden down all them that err from thy statutes: for their deceit is falsehood.

Thou puttest away all the wicked of the earth like dross: therefore I love thy testimonies.

My flesh trembleth for fear of thee; and I am afraid of thy judgments.

I have done judgment and justice: leave me not to mine oppressors.

Be surety for thy servant for good: let not the proud oppress me.

Mine eyes fail for thy salvation, and for the word of thy righteousness.

Deal with thy servant according unto thy mercy, and teach me thy statutes.

I am thy servant; give me understanding, that I may know thy testimonies.

It is time for thee, LORD, to work: for they have made void thy law.

Therefore I love thy commandments above gold; yea, above fine gold.

Therefore I esteem all thy precepts concerning all things to be right; and I hate every false way.

Thy testimonies are wonderful: therefore doth my soul keep them.

The entrance of thy words giveth light; it giveth understanding unto the simple.

I opened my mouth, and panted: for I longed for thy commandments.

Look thou upon me, and be merciful unto me, as thou usest to do unto those that love thy name.

Order my steps in thy word: and let not any iniquity have dominion over me.

Deliver me from the oppression of man: so will I keep thy precepts.

Make thy face to shine upon thy servant; and teach me thy statutes.

Rivers of waters run down mine eyes, because they keep not thy law.

Righteous art thou, O LORD, and upright are thy judgments.

Thy testimonies that thou hast commanded are righteous and very faithful.

My zeal hath consumed me, because mine enemies have forgotten thy words.

Thy word is very pure: therefore thy servant loveth it.

I am small and despised: yet do not I forget thy precepts.

Thy righteousness is an everlasting righteousness, and thy law is the truth.

Trouble and anguish have taken hold on me: yet thy commandments are my delights.

The righteousness of thy testimonies is everlasting: give me understanding, and I shall live.

I cried with my whole heart; hear me, O LORD; I will keep thy statutes.

I cried unto thee; save me, and I shall keep thy testimonies.

I prevented the dawning of the morning, and cried: I hoped in thy word.

Mine eyes prevent the night watches, that I might meditate in thy word.

Hear my voice according unto thy lovingkindness: O LORD, quicken me according to thy judgment.

They draw nigh that follow after mischief: they are far from thy law.

Thou art near, O LORD; and all thy commandments are truth.

Concerning thy testimonies, I have known of old that thou hast founded them for ever.

Consider mine affliction, and deliver me: for I do not forget thy law.

Plead my cause, and deliver me: quicken me according to thy word.

Salvation is far from the wicked: for they seek not thy statutes.

Great are thy tender mercies, O LORD: quicken me according to thy judgments.

Many are my persecutors and mine enemies; yet do I not decline from thy testimonies.

I beheld the transgressors, and was grieved; because they kept not thy word.

Consider how I love thy precepts: quicken me, O LORD, according to thy lovingkindness.

Thy word is true from the beginning: and every one of thy righteous judgments endureth for ever.

Princes have persecuted me without a cause: but my heart standeth in awe of thy word.

I rejoice at thy word, as one that findeth great spoil.

I hate and abhor lying: but thy law do I love.

Seven times a day do I praise thee, because of thy righteous judgments.

Great peace have they which love thy law: and nothing shall offend them.

LORD, I have hoped for thy salvation, and done thy commandments.

My soul hath kept thy testimonies; and I love them exceedingly.

I have kept thy precepts and thy testimonies: for all my ways are before thee.

Let my cry come near before thee, O LORD: give me understanding according to thy word.

Let my supplication come before thee: deliver me according to thy word.

My lips shall utter praise, when thou hast taught me thy statutes.

My tongue shall speak of thy word: for all thy commandments are righteousness.

Let thine hand help me; for I have chosen thy precepts.

I have longed for thy salvation, O LORD; and thy law is my delight.

Let my soul live, and it shall praise thee; and let thy judgments help me.

I have gone astray like a lost sheep: seek thy servant; for I do not forget thy commandments.

MY PRAYER LIST

_____
_____
_____
_____
_____
_____
_____
_____
_____
_____
_____
_____
_____
_____
_____
_____
_____
_____
_____
_____
_____
_____
_____
_____
_____
_____
_____
_____
_____
_____
_____

MY PRAYER LIST

MY PRAYER LIST

_____

_____

_____

_____

_____

_____

_____

_____

_____

_____

_____

_____

_____

_____

_____

_____

_____

_____

_____

_____

_____

_____

_____

_____

_____

_____

_____

_____

_____

_____

_____

MY PRAYER LIST

MY PRAYER LIST

MY PRAYER LIST

_____
_____
_____
_____
_____
_____
_____
_____
_____
_____
_____
_____
_____
_____
_____
_____
_____
_____
_____
_____
_____
_____
_____
_____
_____
_____
_____
_____
_____
_____
_____
_____

MY PRAYER LIST

_____
_____
_____
_____
_____
_____
_____
_____
_____
_____
_____
_____
_____
_____
_____
_____
_____
_____
_____
_____
_____
_____
_____
_____
_____
_____
_____
_____
_____

MY PRAYER LIST

_____

_____

_____

_____

_____

_____

_____

_____

_____

_____

_____

_____

_____

_____

_____

_____

_____

_____

_____

_____

_____

_____

_____

_____

_____

_____

_____

_____

MY PRAYER LIST

_____
_____
_____
_____
_____
_____
_____
_____
_____
_____
_____
_____
_____
_____
_____
_____
_____
_____
_____
_____
_____
_____
_____
_____
_____
_____
_____
_____
_____
_____

MY PRAYER LIST

PERSONAL STUDY NOTES

PERSONAL STUDY NOTES

PERSONAL STUDY NOTES

PERSONAL STUDY NOTES

_____
_____
_____
_____
_____
_____
_____
_____
_____
_____
_____
_____
_____
_____
_____
_____
_____
_____
_____
_____
_____
_____
_____
_____
_____
_____
_____
_____
_____

PERSONAL STUDY NOTES

PERSONAL STUDY NOTES

PERSONAL STUDY NOTES

PERSONAL STUDY NOTES

PERSONAL STUDY NOTES

PERSONAL STUDY NOTES